Charles Godfrey Leland

Hans Breitmann's Ballads

Charles Godfrey Leland

Hans Breitmann's Ballads

ISBN/EAN: 9783742875242

Manufactured in Europe, USA, Canada, Australia, Japa

Cover: Foto ©ninafisch / pixelio.de

Manufactured and distributed by brebook publishing software (www.brebook.com)

Charles Godfrey Leland

Hans Breitmann's Ballads

Contents.

	PAGE
HANS BREITMANN'S PARTY,	5
BREITMANN IN BATTLE,	7
BREITMANN IN MARYLAND,	12
BREITMANN AS A BUMMER,	17
BREITMANN IN KANSAS,	22
DIE SCHŒNE WITTWE. (DE POOTY VIDDER.)	
VOT DE YANKEE CHAP SUNG,	26
HOW DER BREITMANN CUT HIM OUT,	27
BREITMANN AND THE TURNERS,	28
BALLAD,	31
HANS BREITMANN'S CHRISTMAS,	33
DER FREISCHUETZ,	41
HANS BREITMANN ABOUT TOWN,	47
SCHNITZERL'S PHILOSOPEDE—PARDT FIRSDT,	53
SCHNITZERL'S PHILOSOPEDE—PARDT SECONDT,	55
A BALLAD APOUT DE ROWDIES,	67
WEIN GEIST,	69

HANS BREITMANN IN POLITICS:

    I. THE NOMINATION, ... 72
    II. THE COMMITTEE OF INSTRUCTION, . . 75
    III. MR. TWINE EXPLAINS BEING "SOUND UPON THE GOOSE," 78
    IV. HOW BREITMANN AND SCHMIT WERE REPORTED TO BE LOG-ROLLING, . . 83
    V. HOW THEY HELD THE MASS MEETING, . 87
    VI. BREITMANN'S GREAT SPEECH, . . 89
    VII. THE AUTHOR ASSERTS THE VAST INTELLECTUAL SUPERIORITY OF GERMANS TO AMERICANS, ... 95
    VIII. SHOWING HOW MR. HIRAM TWINE "PLAYED OFF" ON SMITH, ... 98

BREITMANN'S GOING TO CHURCH, . . . 107
THE FIRST EDITION OF BREITMANN. SHOWING HOW AND WHY IT WAS THAT IT NEVER APPEARED, ... 121
I GILI ROMANESKRO. A GIPSY BALLAD, . 132
STEINLI VON SLANG. A BALLAD, . . . 135
TO A FRIEND STUDYING GERMAN, . . . 144
LOVE SONG, ... 147
GLOSSARY, ... 149

Hans Breitmann's Party.

Hans Breitmann gife a barty,
    Dey had biano-blayin;
I felled in lofe mit a Merican frau,
    Her name vas Madilda Yane.
She hat haar as prown ash a pretzel,
    Her eyes vas himmel-plue,
Und ven dey looket indo mine,
    Dey shplit mine heart in two.

Hans Breitmann gife a barty,
    I vent dere you'll pe pound.
I valtzet mit Madilda Yane
    Und vent shpinnen round und round.
De pootiest Fraeulein in de House,
    She vayed 'pout dwo hoondred pound,
Und efery dime she gife a shoomp
    She make de vindows sound.

Hans Breitmann gife a barty,
    I dells you it cost him dear.
Dey rolled in more ash sefen kecks
    Of foost-rate Lager Beer.
Und venefer dey knocks de shpicket in
    De Deutschers gifes a cheer.
I dinks dat so vine a barty,
    Nefer coom to a het dis year.

Hans Breitmann gife a barty;
   Dere all vas Souse und Brouse,
Ven de sooper comed in, de gompany
   Did make demselfs to house;
Dey ate das Brot and Gensy broost,
   De Bratwurst and Braten fine,
Und vash der Abendessen down
   Mit four parrels of Neckarwein.

Hans Breitmann gife a barty
   We all cot troonk ash bigs.
I poot mine mout to a parrel of bier
   Und emptied it oop mit a schwigs.
Und denn I gissed Madilda Yane
   Und she shlog me on de kop,
Und de gompany fited mit daple-leeks
   Dill de coonshtable made oos shtop.

Hans Breitmann gife a barty—
   Where ish dat barty now!
Where ish de lofely golden cloud
   Dat float on de moundain's prow?
Where ish de himmelstrahlende Stern—
   De shtar of de shpirit's light?
All goned afay mit de Lager Beer—
   Afay in de ewigkeit!

Breitmann in Battle.

"Tunc tapfre ausfuhrere Streitum et Rittris dignum potuere erjagere lobum."

DER FADER UND DER SON.

I dinks I'll go a fitin—outspoke der Breitemann,
"It's eighdeen hoonderd fordy eight since I kits
    swordt in hand;
Dese fourdeen years mit Hecker all roostin I haf been,
Boot now I kicks der Teufel oop and goes for
    sailin in."

"If you go land out-ridin," said Caspar Pickletongue,
"Foost ding you knows you cooms across some repels
    prave and young,
Away down Sout' in Tixey, dey'll split you like a
    clam"—
"For dat," spoke out der Breitmann, "I doos not
    gare one tam,

Who der Teufel pe's de repels und vhere dey kits deir
    sass,
If dey make a run on Breitmann he'll soon let out de
    gas;
I'll shplit dem like kartoffels: I'll slog em on de kop;
I'll set de plackguarts roonin so dey don't know vhere
    to shtop."

Und den outshpoke der Breitmann, mit his schlaeger py
    his side :
" Forvarts, my pully landsmen ! it's dime to run und
    ride ;
Will riden, will fighten—der Copitain I'll pe,   [ric !"
It's sporn und horn und saddle now—all in de Cavall-

Und ash dey rode troo Winchester, so herrlich to pe
    seen,
Dere coomed some repel cavallrie a riden on de creen ;
Mit a sassy repel Dootchman—an colonel in gommand :
Says he, " Vot Teufel makes you here in dis mein
    Faderland ?

" You're dressed oop like a shentleman mit your plack-
    guard Yankee crew,
You mudsills and meganics ! Der Teufel put you troo !
Old Yank you ought to shtay at home und dake your
    liddle horn,
Mit some oldt voomans for a noorse"—der Breitmann
    laugh mit shkorn.

" Und should I trink mein lager-bier und roost mine
    self to home ?   [thoom :
Ife got too many dings like you to mash beneat' my
In many a fray und fierce foray dis Deutschman will be
    feared   [his peard."
Pefore he stops dis vightin trade—'twas dere he greyed

" I pools dat peard out by de roots—I gifes him sooch
    a dwist   [tionist !
Dill all de plood roons out, you tamned old Apoli-
Your creenpacks mit your swordt und watch right ofer
    you moost shell,   [h–ll !"
Und den you goes to Libby straight—und after dat to

" Mein creenpacks und mein schlaeger, I kits 'em in
    New York,   [talk ;"
To gife dem up to creenhorns, young man, is not de
De heroes shtopped deir sassin' here und grossed deir
    sabres dwice,
Und de vay dese Deutschers vent to vork vos von pig
    ding on ice.

Der younger fetch de older such a gottallmachty smack
Der Breitmann dinks he really hears his skool go shplit
    und crack ;
Der repel choomps dwelfe paces back, und so he safe
    his life :
Der Breitmann says : " I guess dem choomps you
    learns dem of your vife."

" If I should learn of vomans I dinks it vere a shame,
Bei Gott I am a shentleman, aristograt, and game.
My fader vos anoder—I lose him fery young—
Ter teufel take your soul ! Coom on ! I'll split your
    waggin' tongue !"

A Yankee drick der Breitmann dried—dat oldt gray-
    pearded man—   [he ran.
For ash the repel raised his swordt, beneat' dat swordt
All roundt der shlim yoong repel's waist his arms oldt
    Breitmann pound,
Und shlinged him down oopon his pack und laidt him
    on der ground.

" Who rubs against olt kittle-pots may keep vite—if he
    can,   [man ?
Say vot you dinks of vightin now mit dis old shentle-
Your dime is oop; you got to die, und I your breest
    vill pe ;
Peliev'st dou in Morál Ideas ? If so I lets you free."

" I don't know nix apout Ideas—no more dan pout
    Saint Paul,
Since I peen down in Tixey I kits no books at all ;
I'm greener ash de clofer-grass ; I'm shtupid as a
    shpoon ;
I'm ignoranter ash de nigs—for dey takes de *Tribune*.

" Mein fader's name vas Breitmann, I heard mein mut-
    ter say,
She read de bapers dat he died after she rooned afay ;
Dey say he leaf some broperty—berhaps 'twas all a
    sell—
If I could lay mein hands on it I likes it mighty well."

"Und vas dy fader Breitmann? *Bist du* his kit und kin?
Denn know dat *ich* der Breitmann dein lieber Vater bin?"
Der Breitmann poolled his hand-shoe off und shooked
    him py de hand;
"Ve'll hafe some trinks on strengt of dis—or else may
    I pe tam'd!"

"Oh! fader, how I shlog your kop," der younger
    Breitmann said;
"I'd den dimes sooner had it coom right down on mine
    own headt!"
"Oh, never mind—dat soon dry oop—I shticks him mit
    a blaster;   [der."
If I had shplit you like a fish, dat vere an vorse tisas-

Dis fight did last all afternoon—*wohl* to de fesper tide,
Und droo de streeds of Vinchesder, der Breitmann he
    did ride.   [tory!
Vot vears der Breitmann on his hat? De ploom of fie-
Who's dat a ridin' py his side? "Dis here's mein son,"
    says he.

How stately rode der Breitmann oop!—how lordly he
    kit down?   [prown!
How glorious from de great *pokal* he drink de bier so
But der Yunger bick der parrel oop und schwig him
    all at one.   [mein son!"
"Bei Gott! dat settles all dis dings—I *know* dou art

Der one has got a fader; de oder found a child.
Bote ride oopon one war-path now in pattle fierce und
    wild.
It makes so glad our hearts to hear dat dey did so suc-
    ceed—
Und damit hat sein' Ende DES JUNGEN BREITMANN'S
    LIED.

Breitmann in Maryland.

DER Breitmann mit his gompany,
    Rode out in Marylandt.
"Dere's nichts to trink in dis countrie;
    Mine troat's as dry as sand.
It's light canteen und haversack,
    It's hoonger mixed mit doorst;
Und if we had some lager-bier
    I'd trink oontil I boorst.
      Gling, glang, gloria!
We'd trink oontil we boorst.

"Herr Leut'nant, take a dozen men,
  Und ride dis land around!
Herr Feldwebel, go foragin'
  Dill somedings goot is found.
Gotts-doonder! men, go ploonder!
  We hafn't trinked a bit
Dis fourdeen hours! If I had bier
  I'd sauf oontil I shplit!
    Gling, glang, gloria!
  We'd sauf oontil we shplit!"

At mitternacht a horse's hoofs
  Coom rattlin' troo de camp;
"Rouse dere!—coom rouse der house dere!
  Herr Copitain—we moost tromp!
De scouds have found a repel town,
  Mit repel davern near,
A repel keller in de cround,
  Mit repel lager bier!!
    Gling, glang, gloria!
  All fool of lager-bier!

Gottsdonnerkreuzschockschwerenoth!
  How Breitmann broked de bush!
"O let me see dat lager bier!
  O let me at him rush!
Und is mein sabre sharp und true,
  Und is mein war-horse goot?

To get one quart of lager bier
   I'd shpill a sea of ploot.
      Gling, glang, gloria!
   I'd shpill a sea of ploot.

" Fuenf hoonderd repels hold de down,
   One hoonderd strong are we;
Who gares a tam for all de odds
   Wenn men so dirsty pe."
And in dey smashed and down dey crashed,
   Like donder-polts dey fly,
Rush fort as der wild yæger cooms
   Mit blitzen troo de shky.
      Gling, glang, gloria!
   Like blitzen troo de shky.

How flewed to rite, how flewd to left
   De moundains, drees unt hedge;
How left und rite de yæger corps
   Went donderin troo de pridge.
Und splash und splosh dey ford de shtream
   Where not some pridges pe:
All dripplin in de moondlight peam
   Stracks went de cavallrie!
      Gling, glang, gloria!
   Der Breitmann's cavallrie.

Und hoory, hoory on dey rote,
    Oonheedin vet or try ;
Und horse und rider shnort und blowed,
    Und shparklin bepples fly.
Ropp ! ropp ! I shmell de barley-prew !
    Dere's somedings goot ish near
Ropp ! Ropp !—I scent de kneiperei ;
    We've got to lager bier !
        Gling, glang gloria !
    We've got to lager bier !

Hei ! how de carpine pullets klinged
    Oopon de helmets hart !
Oh, Breitmann—how dy sabre ringed ;
    Du alter Knasterbart !
De contrapands dey sing for choy
    To see de rebs go down,
Und hear der Breitmann grimly gry :
    Hoorah !—we've dook de down.
        Gling, glang, gloria !
        Victoria, victoria !
    De Dootch have dook de down.

Mid shout and crash and sabre flash,
    And wild husaren shout
De Dootchmen boorst de keller in,
    Unt rolled de lager out ;

And in the coorlin powder shmoke,
   While shtill de pullets sung.
Dere shtood der Breitmann, axe in hand,
   A knockin out de boong.
      Gling, glang, gloria !
      Victoria ! Encoria !
   De shpicket beats de boong.

Gotts ! vot a shpree der Breitmann had
   While yet his hand was red,
A trinkin lager from his poots
   Among de repel tead.
'Twas dus dey went at mitternight
   Along der moundain side ;
'Twas dus dey help make history !
   Dis was der Breitmann's ride.
      Gling, glang, gloria ;
      Victoria ! Victoria !
      Cer'visia, encoria ?
   De treadful mitnight ride
Of Breitmann's wild Freischarlinger,
   All famous, broad, und wide.

Breitmann as a Bummer.

DER Sheneral Sherman holts oop on his coorse.
　　He shtops at de gross-road und reins in his horse.
　"Dere's a ford on de rifer dis day we moost dake,
Or elshe de grand army in bieces shall preak!"
Ven shoost ash dis vord from his lips had gone bast,
　There coomed a young orterly gallopin fast,
Who gry mit amazement: "Here Shen'ral! Goot Lord!
　Dat bummer der Breitmann ish holdin der ford!"

Der Shen'ral he ootered no hymn und no psalm,
　But opened his lips und he priefly say "D——n!
Dere moost hafe been viskey on dat side der rifer;
　To get it dose shaps would set hell in a shiver,
But now dat dey hold it, ride quick to deir aid:
　Ho Sickles! move promp'ly, send down a prigade
Dat Dootchman moost work mighty hard mit his sword
　If againsd a whole army he holds to de ford."

Dey spoored on, dey hoory'd on, gallopin shtraight,
　But for Breitmann help coomed shust a liddle too late,
For ash de Lauwiné goes smash mit her pound,
　So on to de Bummers de repels coom down:
Heinrich von Schinkenstein's tead in de road,
　Dieterich Hinkelbein's flat ash a toad;
Und Sepperl—Tyroler—shpoke nefer a vord,
　But shoost "*Mutter Gottes!*"—und died in de ford.

Itsch'l of Innspruck ish drilled troo de hair,
    Einer aus Bœblingen—he too vash dere—
Karli of Karlisruh's shot near de fence,
    (His horse vash o'erloadet mit toorkies und hens,)
Und dough he like a ravin mad cannibal fought,
    Yet der Breitmann—der capt'n—der hero vash caught;
Und de last dings ve saw, he was tied mit a cord,
    For de repels had goppled him oop at de ford.

Dey shtripped off his goat und skyugled his poots,
    Dey dressed him mit rags of a repel recruits;
But von grey-haared oldt veller shmiled crimly und bet
    Dat Breitman vouldt pe a pad egg for dem, yet.
"He has more on his pipe as dem vellers allows;
    He has cardts yet in hand und *das Spiel ist nicht aus*,
Dey'll find dat dey took in der teufel to board,
    De day dey pooled Breitmann well ofer de ford."

In de Bowery each bier-haus mit crape vas oop-done,
    Ven dey read in de bapers dat Breitmann vas gone;
Und de Dootch all cot troonk oopon lager und wein,
    At the great Trauer-fest of de Toorner Verein
Dere vas wein-en mit weinen ven beoples did dink
    Dat Sherman's great Sherman cood nefer more trink.
Und in Villiam Shtreet veepin und vailen vas hoor'd,
    Pecause der Hans Breitmann vas lost at de ford.

SECONDT PARDT.

In dulce jubilo now ve all sings,
   A-waivin de panners like avery dings.
  De preeze troo de bine-drees ish cooler und salt,
   Und der Shen'ral is merry venefer ve hait;
Loosty und merry he schmells at de preeze,
   Lustig und heiter he looks troo de drees,
Lustig und heiter ash vell he may pe,
   For Sherman, at last, has marched down to the sea!

Dere's a gry from de guart—dere's a clotter und dramp,
   Ven dat fery same orterly rides troo de camp,
Who report on de ford. Dere ish droples and awe
   In de face of de youf' apout somedings he saw;
Und he shpeak me in Fræntsch, like he always do:
   "Look! [his spook!
   Sagre pleu! fentre Tieu!—dere ish Breitmann—
He ish goming dis way! *Nom de garce!* can it pe
   Dat de spooks of te tead men coom down to de sea!"

Und ve looks, und ve sees, und ve tremples mit tread,
   For risin' all swart on de efenin red
Vas Johannes—der Breitmann—der war es, bei Gott!
   Coom ridin' to oos-ward, right shtrait to de shpot!
All mouse-still ve shtood, yet mit oop-shoompin hearts,
   For he look shoost so pig ash de shiant of de Hartz;
Und I heard de Sout Deutschers say "Ave Morie!
   Braise Gott all goot shpirids py land und py sea!"

Boot Itzig of Frankfort he lift oop his nose,
    Und be-mark dat de shpook hat peen changin his
        clothes,
For he seemed like an Generalissimus drest
    In a vlamin new coat and magnificent vest.
Six bistols beschlagen mit silber he wore,
    Und a gold mounted swordt like an Kaisar he bore,
Und ve dinks dat de ghosdt—or votever he pe—
    Moost hafe proken some panks on his vay to de sea.

"Id is he!" "*Und er lebt noch!* he lifes," ve all say:
    Der Breitmann—Oldt Breitmann!—Hans Breit-
        mann! *Herr Je!*"
Und ve roosh to emprace him, and shtill more ve find
    Dat vherefer he'd peen, he'd left noding pehind.
In bote of his poots dere vas porte-moneys crammed,
    Mit creen-packs stoof full all his haversack jammed,
In his bockets cold dollars were shinglin' deir doons
    Mit two doozen votches und four doozen shpoons,
Und dwo silber tea-pods for makin' his dea,
    Der ghosdt hafe pring mit him, *en route* to de sea.

Mit goot sweed-botatoes, und doorkies, und rice,
    Ve makes him a sooper of avery dings nice.
Und de bummers hoont roundt apout, *alle wie ein*,
    Dill dey findt a plantaschion mit parrels of wein.

Den t'vas "here's to you, Breitmann! Alt Schwed'—
   bist zuruck?
  Vot teufels you makes since dis fourteen nights
     week?"
Und ve holds von shtupendous und derriple shpree
  For choy dat der Breitmann has got to de sea.

But in fain tid ve ashk vhere der Breitmann hat peen,
  Vot he tid; vot he pass troo—or vot he might seen?
Vhere he kits his vine horse, or who gafe him dem
     woons,
Und how Brovidence plessed him mit tea-pods und
     shpoons?
For to all of dem queeries he only reblies
  "If you dells me no quesdions, I ashks you no lies!"
So 'twas glear dat some derriple mysh'dry moost pe
  Vhere he kits all dat ploonder he prings to de sea.

Dere ish bapers in Richmond dells derriple lies
  How Sherman's grand armee hafe raise deir sooplies:
For ve readt *in brindt* dat der Sheneral Grant
  Say de bummers hafe only shoost dake vat dey vant.
But 'tis vhispered dat vhile a refolfer'll go round
  Der BREITMANN vill nefer a peggin' be found;
Or shtarvin' ash brisner—by doonder!—not he,
  Vhile der teufel could help him to ged to de sea.

Breitmann in Kansas.

V ONCE oopon a dimes, goot vhile afder der war vas ofer, der Herr Breitmann vent oud West, drafellin apout like afery dings—"*circuivit terram et perambulavit eam,*" ash der Tyfel said ven dey ask him : " how vash you and how you has peen ?" Von efenings he vas drafel mit some ladies und shendlemans, und he shtaid *incognitus.* Und dey singed songs, dill py und py one of de ladies say : " Ish any podies here ash know de crate pallad of Hans Breitmann's Barty ?" Den Haus say : " *Ecce Gallus!* I am dat rooster !" Den der Hans dook a trink und a let-bencil und a biece of baper, and goes indo himself a little dimes und denn coomes out again mit dis boem :

> Hans Breitmann vent to Kansas;
>   He drafel fast und far.
> He rided shoost drei dousand miles
>   All in von rail-roat car.
> He knowed foost rate how far he goed—
>   He gounted all de vile.
> Dere vash shoost one bottle of champagne,
>   Dat bopped at efery mile.
>
> Hans Breitmann vent to Kansas;
>   I dell you vot my poy.
> You bet dey hat a pully dimes
>   In crossin Illinoy.

Dey speaked dere speaks to all de folk
    A shtandin in de car;
Den ask dem in to dake a trink,
    Und corned em *ganz und gar*.

Hans Breitmann vent to Kansas;
    By shings! dey did it prown.
Ven he cot into Leafenvort,
    He found himself in town.
Dey dined him at de Blanter's House,
    More goot as man could dink;
Mit avery dings on cart to eat,
    Und dwice as mooch to trink.

Hans Breitmann vent to Kansas;
    He vent it on de loud.
At Ellsvort, in de prairie land,
    He foundt a pully crowd.
He looked for bleedin' Kansas,
    But dat's " blayed out," dey say;
De whisky keg's de only dings
    Dat's bleedin' der to-day.

Hans Breitmann vent to Kansas,
    To see vot he could hear.
He foundt soom Deutschers dat exisdt
    Py makin' lager bier.

Says he: "*Wie gehts du Alt Gesell?*"
   But no dings could be heard;
Dey'd growed so fat in Kansas
   Dat dey couldn't speak a vord.

Hans Breitmann vent to Kansas;
   Py shings! I dell you vot.
Von day he met a crisly bear
   Dat rooshed him down, *bei Gott!*
Boot der Breitmann took und bind der bear,
   Und bleased him fery much—
For efery vordt der crisly growled
   Vas goot Bavarian Dutch!

Hans Breitmann vent to Kansas!
   By donder dat is so!
He ridet out upon de plains
   To shase de boofalo.
He fired his rifle at the bools,
   Und gallop troo de shmoke,
Und shoomp de canyons shoost as if
   Der tyfel vas a choke!

It's hey de trail to Santa Fe;
   It's ho! agross de plain.
It's lope along de Denver road,
   Until we toorn again.

Und de railroad dravel after us
  Apout as quick as we;
Dis Kansas ish de fastest land
  Ash efer I did see.

Hans Breitmann vent to Kansas;
  He have a pully dime;
Bu 'tvas in oldt Missouri
  Dat dey rooshed him up sublime.
Dey took him to der Bilot Nob,
  Und all der nobs around;
Dey spreed him und dey tea'd him
  Dill dey roon him to de ground.

Hans Breitmann vent to Kansas;
  Troo all dis earthly land,
A vorkin out life's mission here
  Soobyectifly und grand.
Some beoblesh runs de beautiful,
  Some works philosophic;
Der Breitmann solfe de infinide
  Ash von eternal shpree!

Die Schœne Wittwe.

(DE POOTY VIDDER.)

Vot de Yankee Chap sung.

"DAT pooty liddle vidder
    Vot we dosh'nt vish to name,
  Ish still leben on dat liddle shtreet,
    A-doin' shuss de same.
De glerks aroundt de gorners
    Somedimes goes round to zee
How die tarlin liddle vitchy ees,
    Und ask 'er how she pe.
Dey lofes her ver' goot liquœr,
    Dey lofes her liddle shtore;
Dey lofes her liddle paby,
    But dey lofes die vidder more.
To dalk mit dat shveet vidder,
    Ven she hands das lager round,
Vill make der shap dat does id
    Pe happy, ve'll be pound.
Dat ish if ve can vell pelieve
    De glerks vat drinks das peer,
Who goes in dere for noding elshe,
    Put simply for to zee her."

How der Breitmann cut him out.

Oh yes I know die wittwe,
    Mit eyes so prite und proun!
    She's de allerschœnste wittwe
Vot live in dis here town.
In her plack silk gown—mine grashious!—
    All puttoned to de neck—
Und a pooty liddle collar,
    Mitout a shpot or shpeck.
Ho! clear de drack you oder *fraus*—
    You cant pegin to shine
Ven de lofely vidder cooms along—
    Dis vidder ash ish mine!
Ho! clear de drack you Yankee chaps,
    You Englishers und sooch.
You cant pegin to coot me out,
    Mit out you dalks in Dootch.
Ich hab die schœne wittwe
    Schon lange nit gesehn,
Ich sah sie gestern Abend
    Wohl bei dem Counter stehn.
Die Wangen rein wie Milch und Blut,
    Die Augen hell und klar.
Ich hab sie sechsmal auch gekusst—
    Potztausend! das ist wahr.

Breitmann and the Turners.

HANS BREITMANN choined de Turners
    Novemper in de fall,
  Und dey gifed a boostin' bender
All in de Toorner Hall.
Dere coomed de whole Gesangverein
    Mit der Liederlich Aepfel Chor,
Und dey blowed on de drooms und stroomed
    on de fifes
Till dey couldn't refife no more.

Hans Breitmann choined de Toorners,
    Dey all set oop some shouts,
Dey took'd him into deir Toorner Hall,
    Und poots him a course of shprouts,
Dey poots him on de barrell-hell pars
    Und shtands him oop on his head,
Und dey poomps de beer mit an enchine hose
    In his mout' dill he's 'pout half tead!

Hans Breitmann choined de Toorners;—
    Dey make shimnastig dricks
He stoot on de middle of de floor,
    Und put oop a fifdy-six.
Und den he trows it to de roof,
    Und schwig off a treadful trink:
De veight coom toomple pack on his headt,
    Und py shinks! he didn't vink!

Hans Breitmann choined de Toorners :—
    Mein Gott! how dey drinked und shwore
Dere vas Schwabians und Tyrolers,
    Und Bavarians by de score.
Some vellers coomed from de Rheinland,
    Und Frankfort-on-de-Main,
Boot dere vas only von Sharman dere,
    Und *he* vas a *Holstein* Dane.

Hans Breitmann choined de Toorners,
    Mit a Limpurg' cheese he coom;
Ven he open de box it schmell so loudt
    It knock de musik doomb.
Ven de Deutschers kit de flavor,
    It coorl de haar on dere head;
Boot dere vas dwo Amerigans dere;
    Und, py tam! it kilt dem dead!

Hans Breitmann choined de Toorners;
    De ladies coomed in to see;
Dey poot dem in de blace for de gals,
    All in der gal-lerie.
Dey ashk: "Vhere ish der Breitmann?"
    And dey dremple mit awe and fear
Ven dey see him schwingen py de toes,
    A trinken lager bier.

Hans Breitmann choined de Toorners :—
  I dells you vot py tam!
Dey sings de great Urbummellied :
  De holy Sharman psalm.
Und ven dey kits to de gorus
  You ought to hear dem dramp!
It scared der Teufel down below
  To hear de Dootchmen stamp.

Hans Breitmann choined de Toorners :—
  By Donner! it vas grand,
Vhen de whole of dem goes a valkin'
  Und dancin' on dere hand,
Mit de veet all wavin' in de air,
  Gottstausend! vot a dricks!
Dill der Breitmann fall und dey all go down
  Shoost like a row of bricks.

Hans Breitmann choined de Toorners,
  Dey lay dere in a heap,
And slept dill de early sonnen shine
  Come in at de window creep;
And de preeze it vake dem from deir dream,
  And dey go to kit deir feed :
Here hat' dis song an Ende—
  Das ist DES BREITMANNSLIED.

Ballad.

Der noble Ritter Hugo
    Von Schwillensaufenstein,
  Rode out mit shpeer and helmet,
    Und he coom to de panks of de Rhine.

Und oop dere rose a meer maid,
  Vot hadn't got nodings on,
Und she say, "Oh, Ritter Hugo,
  Vhere you goes mit yourself alone?"

And he says, "I rides in de creenwood
  Mit helmet und mit shpeer,
Till I cooms into em Gasthaus,
  Und dere I trinks some beer."

Und den outshpoke de maiden
  Vot hadn't got nodings on:
"I tont dink mooch ot beoplesh
  Dat goes mit demselfs alone.

"You'd petter coom down in de wasser,
  Vere deres heaps of dings to see,
Und hafe a shplendid tinner
  Und drafel along mit me.

"Dere you sees de fisch a schwimmin,
    Und you catches dem efery one :"—
So sang dis wasser maiden
    Vot hadn't got nodings on.

"Dere ish drunks all full mit money
    In ships dat vent down of old;
Und you helpsh yourself, by dunder!
    To shimmerin crowns of gold.

"Shoost look at dese shpoons und vatches!
    Shoost see dese diamant rings!
Coom down und full your bockets,
    Und I'll giss you like avery dings.

"Vot you vantsh mit your schnapps und lager?
    Coom down into der Rhine!
Der ish pottles der Kaiser Charlemagne
    Vonce filled mit gold-red wine!"

Dat fetched him—he shtood all shpell pound;
    She pooled his coat-tails down,
She drawed him oonder der wasser,
    De maidens mit nodings on.

Hans Breitmann's Christmas.

*"Hæc est illa bona dies
Et vocata lætæ quies
Vina sitientibus.*

*"Nullus metus, nec labores,
Nulla cura, nec dolores,
Sint in hoc symposio."*

[*De Generibus Ebriosorum, Francoforti ad Mœnum, A. D.* 1565.]

ID vas on Weihnachtsabend—vot Ghristmas Efe dey call—
Der Breitmann mit his Breitmen tid rent de Musik Hall;
Ash de Breitmen und die vomen who were in de Liederkranz
Vouldt plend deir souls in harmonie to have a bleasin tantz.

Dey reefed de Hall 'mid pushes so nople to be seen,
Aroundt Beethoven's buster dey on-did a garlandt creen;
De laties vork like tyfels two days to scroob de vloor,
Und hanged a crate serenity mit Willkomm! oop de toor!

Und vhile dere vas a Schwein-blatt whose redakteur tid say:
Dat Breitmann he vas liederlich vet antworded dis-away,
Ve maked anoder serenity mid ledders plue und red:
" Our Leader lick de repels! N. G." (enof gesaid.)

Und anoder serene dransparency ve make de veller baint,
Boot de vay he potch und vertyfeled it vas enof to shvear a saint,

5   (33)

For ve vanted La Germania—boot der ardist mit a
bloonder
Vent und vlorished Lager agross id—und denn poot
Mania oonder!

Und as Ghristmas Efe was gekommen de beoples weren
im Hall,
I shvears you id vas Gott-full—dat sh'plendit, pe-glo-
ried ball?
Ve hat foon wie der Teufel in Frankreich—we coot oop
like ter tyfel in France,
Und valk pair-wise in, while de musik blayed loudt de
Fackel-Tanz.

But ven de valtz shtrike oopwart we most went out of fits,
Ash der Breitmann led off on a dwister mid de lofely
Helmina Schmitz.
He valtz shoost like he vas shtandin shtill, mit a peau-
diful solemn shmile,
Und 'Mina say he nafer shtop poussiren allaweil.

"Es tœnt, es rauschet Saitenklang—I hear de musik
call
Den kerzenhellen Saal entlang—all troo de gleamin
Hall,
O mœcht ich schweben stolz und froh—O mighdt I
efer pe
Mit dir durchs ganze Leben so!—my Lebenlang by dee."

Und faster play de musik de Wellen und Wogen von
  Strauss;
Und some drop into de tantzen und some of dem drop
  aus;
Und soon like a shtorm in de Meere I feel de reelin vloor,
So de shpinners shtop mit de shpinsters, for dey couldn't
  shpin no more.

Now weren ve all frolic, und lauter guter ding,
Und dirsty ash a broosh-pinder—ven ve hear some
  glæsses ring;
Foorst mild und sonft in de distants—like de song of a
  nightingoll,
Den a ringin und rottlin und clotterin—ash de Gluck
  of Edenhall?

Hei! how we roosh on de liquor!—hei! how de kell-
  ners coom!
Hei! how we busted de bier kegs und poonished de
  Punsch a la Rhum,
Like lonely wafes at mitternight oopon some shiant
  shore;
Like an awful shtorm in de Wælder—was de dirsty
  Deutschers' roar!

I pyed some carts for a dime abiece—I pyed shoost
  fifdy-dwo.
Dey were goot for bier, or schnapps, or wein—py donder how dey flew!

I ring de deck on de vaiters for liquor hot und cool,
Und avery dime I blays a cart, py shings, I rake de
 pool!
Und ash ve trinked so comforble, like boogs in any roog,
De trompets blowed *tan da ra dei,* und dere coom in a
 Maskenzug,
A peaudiful brocession, soul-raisin und sooplime,
De marmorbilds of de heroes of de early Sherman dime.

Dere vent der gross Arminius, mit his frau Thusnelda,
 too,
De vellers ash lam de Romans dill dey roon mit noses
 plue,
Den vollowed Quinctilius Varus, who carry a Roman
 yoke,
Und arm-in-arm mit Gambrinus come der Allemane
 Chroc.

Der alte Friedrich Rothbart, und Kaiser Karl der crate,
Mit Roland und Uliverus ven shveepin on in shtate ;
Und Conradin whose sad-full deat' shtill makes our
 heartsen pleed,
Und all of dem oldt vellers aus dem Niblungen Lied.

Und as dey mofed on, der Breitmann maked a tyfeled
 shplendid witz
In anti-word to dis quesdion from de lofely 'Mina
 Schmitz :

"Vy ish id dey always makes in shtone dem vellers so
andiquatet?"
"Vy—dey set in de laps of Ages dill dey got lapi-
dated!"

Und shoost ash de last of dis hisdory hat fonished troo
de toor,
Ve heardt a ge-screech, und Pelz Nickel coom howlin
on de vloor;
Den de laties yell like der tyfel, und vly like gulls mit
vings,
Und der Peltz Nickel lick em mit svitches und ve
laughed like averydings.

I nefer hafe sooch laughen before dat I was geborn,
Und Pelz Nickel ven 'twas ober he blow on a yæger horn
Und denounce do all de beople gesembled in de hall:
Dat a Ghristmas dree vas vaiten mit bresents for oos all!

So ve vollowed him into de zimmer so quick ash dese
vords he said,
To kit dem peaudiful bresents, all gratis und on de dead,
Und in facdt a shplendid Weihnachtsbaum mid lighds
ve druly found,
Und liddel kifts dat ge-kostet a benny abiece all round!

Dere vas Rika Stange die Dessauerinn—a maedchen
shtraigdt und tall,
She got a bicture of Cupid—boot she didn't see it at all

Dill der Breitmann say mit his shplendid shtyle dat all
    de laties dake:
"Dat pend of de bow is de Crecian pend dat you so
    ofden make!"

Anoder scharmante laty, Maria Top, did got
A schwingin mid a ribbon, a liddle benny pot;
Boot Breitmann hafe id de roughest of any oder mans,
For he kit a yellow gratle mit a liddle wooden Hans.

Den next Beethoven's Sinfonie, die orkester did blay;
Adagio—allegro—andante cantabile.
We sat in shtill commotion so dat a bin mighdt drops,
Und de deers roon town der Breitmann's sheeks mit-
    whiles he was trinkin schnapps.

Next dings ve had de Weinnachtstraum gesung by de
    Liederkranz.
Denn I trinked dwelf schoppens of glee wine to sed me
    oop for a tanz;
Dis dimes I tanz wie der Tyfel—we shriek de volk on
    de vloor;
Und boost right indo de sooper room—for ve tanzt a
    hole troo de door!

Denn 'twas rowdy tow und hop-sossa, ve hollered, Mann
    und Weib;
"Rip Sam und sed her oop acain!—ve're all of de
    Shackdaw tribe!"

Venn Pelz Nickel blow his trump once more, und peg
  peg oos to shtop our din,
Und troo de open toor dere comed nine denpins
  marchin in.

Nine vellers tressed like denpins—dey goed to der end'
  der hall,
Und dwo Hans Wurst, shack-puddin glowns—dey rolled
  at em mit a pall.
De palls vas painted peaudiful; dey vas vifdeen feet
  aroundt;
Und de rule of de came: whoefer cot hidt moost doomple on de croundt.

Somedimes dey hit de denpins—somedimes de oder
  volk—
Und pooty soon de gompany was all laid out in shoke;
Boot I tells you vot it makes oos laugh dill ve py nearly
  shplits,
Ven der Breitmann he roll ofer and drip up de Mina
  Schmitz.

Dis lets itself in Sherman pe foost-rade word-blayed on,
Und mongst oos be giftet vellers you pet dat it vas tone!
How der Breitmann mighdt drafel as brideman on de
  roadt dat ish *breit* and *krumm;*
Here de drumpets soundt, and pair-wise ve goed for de
  sooper room.

Ve goed for ge-roasted Welsh-hens, ve goed for ge-
 spickter hare,
Ve goed for kartoffel salade mit butter brod—Kaviar;
Ve roosh at de lordtly sauer-kraut und de wurst vich
 lofely shine,
Und oh mein Gott in Kimmel! how we goed for de
 Mosel-wein!

Und troonker more, und troonker yet, und troonker shtill
 got ve,
In rosy lighdt shtill drivin on agross a fairy see;
Den madder, wilder, frantic-er I proked a salat dish!
Und shoost like roarin elefants ve tanzt aroundt de tish.

I'fe shvimmed in heafenly troonks pefore—boot nefer
 von like dis,
De morgen-het-ache only seemt a bortion of de bliss.
De while in trilling peauty roundt like heafenly vind-
 harps rang
A goosh of golden melodie — de Rhineweinbechers
 Klang.

De meltin minnesingers song—a droonk of honeyd
 rhyme—
De b'wildrin-dipsy Bardic shants of Teutoburgic dime,
Back to de runic dim Valhall und Balder's foamin
 mead;
——Here ents in heller glorie schein des Breitmann's
 Weihnachtslied!

Der Freischuetz.

Wie geht's my frients—if you'll allow.
I sings you rite avay shoost now
Some dretful shdories vitch dey calls
DER FREYSCHUETZ; or, de Magic Balls.

Wohl in Bohemian land it cooms,
Where folks trinks prandy mate of plums;
Dere lifed ein Yager—Maxerl Schmit,
Who shot mit goons and nefer hit.

Und dere vas one old Yager, who
Says, "Maxerl, dis vill nefer do;
If you should miss on trial day,
Dere'l pe de tyfel den to pay.

"If you do miss, you shtupid goose,
Dere'l pe de donnerwetter loose;
For you shant have mine taughter's hand,
Nor pe de Hertshog's yagersmann."

It coomed pefore de day was set,
Dat all de chaps togeder met,
Und Maxerl fired his bix and missed,
Und all de gals cot round and hissed.

Dey laughed pefore, and hissed pehind;
Put one chap, Kaspar, set: "tont mind!
I dells you what, you stuns 'em alls,
If yoost you shoot mit magic palls."

"De magic palls—oh vot is dat!"
"I got dem in mine hoontin hat;
De're plack as kohl und shoot so true,
Oh dems de sort of palls for you.

"You see dat eagle flyin high,
Ein hoondred miles up in de sky?
Shoot at dat eagle mit your bix,
You kills him dead as doonderblix."

"I tont pelieve de dings you say."
"You fool," says Kass, "den plaze avay!"
He plazed avay, ven sure as blood,
Down coomed de eagle in de mud.

"*O was ist das?*" said Maxerl Schmit,
"Vy—dat's de eagle vat you hit.
You kills um vhen you plaze avay;
But dat's a ting you nix ferstay.

"Und you moost go to make dem balls
To de Wolf's Glen ven mitnight falls;
Dow knowst de shpot?—alone and late"—
"O ja—I knows him *ganz* foost-rate."

"But denn I does not likes to go
Among dem dings." Says Kass, "Ach sho!
I'll help you fix dem tyfel chaps;
Like a goot fellow—take some schnapps!

"(*Hilf Zamiel! hilf!*)—Here, trink some more!"
Den Kass vent shtomping roundt de floor,
Und coomed his hoomboogs ofer Schmit,
Till Max said "*Nun—ich gehe mit!*"

All in de finster mitternockt,
When oder folks in shleep vas locked,
Down in de *Wolfsschlucht* Kass did try
His tyfel-strikes und *hexerei*.

Mit skools and pones he made a ring,
De howls and spooks pegin to sing;
Und all de tyfels oonter ground
Coome breaking loose and rushin round.

Den Maxerl cooms along; says he,
"Mein Gott! what dings is dis I see!
I dinks de fery tyfel und all
Moost help to make dem magic pall.

"I vish dat I had nix cum rous,
Und shtaid mineself in bett to house."
"*Hilf Zamiel!*" cried Kass, "you whelp!
You red Dootch tyfel—coom und help!"

Den up dere coomed a tredful shtorm,
De todtengrips aroundt did schwarm;
De howl joomped oop und flapt his vings,
Und turned his het like averydings.

Up troo de groundt here coomed a pot,
Mit leadt und dings to make de shot;
Und hœllisch fire in crimson plaze,
Und awful schmells like Schweitzer **kæs'**.

Across de scene a pine shtick **flew**,
Mit seferal jail-pirds fastent to,
Six treadful jail-birds, mit deir vings
Tied to de shticks mit magic shtrings.

All troo de air, all in a row,
Die wilde Jagd was seen to go;
De hounts und deer all made of pone,
Und hoonted by a skilleton.

Dere coomed de dretful shpectre pig
Who shpitten **fire,** away did dig;
Und fiery drocks und tyfel-snake
A scootin troo de air tid preak.

But Kass he tidn't mind dem alls,
But casted out **de** pullet palls;
Six was to go as dey wouldt like,
De **sevent** moost for de tyfel strike.

At last oopon de trial day
De gals coomed round so nice and gay;
Und denn dey goes and makes a tanz
Und stinged apout de *Jungfernkranz*.

Und denn der Hertshog—dat's de Duke—
Cooms down und dinks he'll take a look;
"Young mans," to Maxerl denn says he,
"Shoost shoot dem dove upon dat dree!"

Denn Maxerl pointed **mit de bix**—
"Potzblitz!" **says** he, "**dat dove I'll fix!**"
He fired his rifle at de *Taub*,
When Kass rolled over in de *Staub*.

De pride she falled too in de dust,
De gals dey cried—de men dey cussed:
De Hertshog says, "It's fery clear
Dat dere has peen some tyfels here;

"**Und** Max has shot mit tyfels-*blei*.
Pfui!—die verfluchte Hexerei!
*O Maximilian! O du
Gehst nit mit rechten Dingen* **zu** *!*"

But den a hermits coomed in late,
Says he, "**I'll** fix dese dings foost-rate."
Und teild de Hertshog dat young men
Will raise **der** tyfel now and denn,

De Duke forgifed de Kaspar dann
Und made of him ein Yagersmann,
What shoots mit bixen gun and pfeil,
Und talks apout de *Waidmannsheil.*

Und denn de pride she coomed to life,
Und cot to pe de Maxerl's wife;
Den all de beoples cried Hoorah!
Das ist recht brav! und hopsasa!

Moral.

Py dis dings may pe oondershtood
Dat vhat is pad vorks ofden goot:
  Or, *Maximilia Maximil-*
  ibus curantur—if you will.

Breitmann about Town.

DER Schwackenhammer coom to down,
    Pefore de Fall vas past,
Und by der Breitmann drawed he in
    Ash dreimals honored gast.
Led's see de sighdts! In self und worldt,—
    Dere's "sighdts" for him, to see,
Who Selbstanschaungsvermœgen hat,
    Said Breitemann, said he.

Dey vented to de Opera Haus,
    Und dere dey vound em blayin'.
Of Offenbach, (der *open brook*,)
    His show spiel Belle Hélène.
"Dere's Offenbach,—Sebastian Bach,—
    Mit Kaulbach,—dat makes dree:
I alvays likes soosh *brooks* ash dese."
    Said Breitemann, said he.

Dey vented to de Bibliothek,
    Vhich Mishder Astor bilt:
Some pooks vere only *en broschure*,
    Und some vere pound und gilt.
"Dat makes de gold—dat makes de *sinn*,
    Mit pooks, ash men, ve see,
De pest tressed vellers gilt de most:"—
    Said Breitemann, said he.

Dey vent to see an edider,
    Who'd shanged his flag und doon,
Und crowed oopon der oder side,
    Dat very afdernoon.
"De anciends vorshipped wetter-cocks.
    To wetter *fanes* pent de knee;
Pow down, mein Schwackenhammer, pow!"
    Said Breitemann, said he.

Dey vented py a panker's hause,
    Und Schwackenhammer shvore,
Id only vant a pig *red shield*
    Hoong oop pefore de toor;
One side of red, one side of gold,
    Like de knighd's in hisdorie—
"De schildern of dat schild is rich,"
    Said Breitemann, said he.

Dey vent oonto a bicture sale,
    Of frames wort' many a cent,
De broberty of a shendleman,
    Who oonto Europe vent.
"Dont gry—he'll soon pe pack again
    Mit anoder gallerie:
He sells dem oud dwelf dimes a year,"
    Said Breitemann, said he.

Dey vented to dis berson's house,
  To see his furnidure,
Sold oud at aucdion rite afay,
  Berembdory und sure.
"He geeps six houses all at vonce
  Each veek a sale dere pe,
Gotts! vat a dime his vife moost hafe!"—
  Said Breitemann, said he.

Dey vent to vind a goot cigar,
  Long dimes dey roamed apout,
Von veller had a pran new sort,
  De fery latest out.
"Mein freund—I dinks you errs yourself
  De shmell ish oldt to me;
De *Infamias Stinkadores* brand,"—
  Said Breitemann, said he.

Dey vented to de *virst* hotel,
  De prandy make dem creep,
A trop of id's enough to make
  A brazen monkey veep.
"Dey say a viner house ash dis,
  Vill soon ge-bildet pe,
Crate Gott!—vot *can* dey mean to trink?"
  Said Breitemann, said he.
    7

Dey vented droo de Irish shtreeds,
    Dey saw vrom haus to haus,
Und gountet oop, 'pout more or less,
    Vive hoondred awful rows.
"If all dese liddle vights dey waste,
    Could *von* crate pattle pe,
Gotts! how de Fenian funds vouldt rise!"
    Said Breitemann, said he.

Dey vent to see de Ridualisds,
    Who vorship Gott mitt vlowers,
In hobes he'll lofe dem pack again,
    In winter among de showers.
"Vhen de Pacific railroat's done
    Dis dings imbrofed vill pe,
De joss-sticks vill pe santal vood,"—
    Said Breitemann, said he.

Dey vent to hear a breecher of
    De last sensadion shtyle,
'Twas 'nough to make der tyfel weep
    To see his "awful shmile."
"Vot bities dat der Fechter ne'er
    Vas in Theologie.
Dey'd make him pishop in dis shoorsh,"
    Said Breitemann, said he.

Dey vent indo a shpordin' crib,
    De rowdies cloostered dick,
Dey ashk him dell dem vot o'glock,
    Und dat infernal quick.
Der Breitmann draw'd his 'volver oud,
    Ash gool ash gool couldt pe,
" Id's shoost a goin' to shdrike six,"
    Said Breitemann, said he.

Dey vent polid'gal meedins next,
    Dey hear dem rant and rail,
Der bresident vas a forger,
    Shoost bardoned oud of jail.
He does it oud of cratitood,
    To dem who set him vree :
" Id's Harmonie of Inderesds,"
    Said Breitemann, said he.

Dey vent to a clairfoyand witch,
    A plack-eyed handsome maid,
She wahrsagt all der vortunes—denn
    " Fife dollars, gents!" she said.
" Dese vitches are nod of dis eart',
    Und yed are *on* id, I see
Der Shakesbeare knew de preed right vell,"
    Said Breitemann, said he.

Dey vented to a restaurand,
 Der vaiter coot a dash ;
He garfed a shicken in a vink,
 Und serfed id at a vlash.
" Dat shap knows vell shoost how to coot,
 Und roon mit poulterie,
He vas copitain oonder Turchin vonce,"
 Said Breitemann, said he.

Dey vented to de Voman's Righds,
 Vere laties all agrees,
De gals should pe de voters,
 Und deir beaux all de votées.
" For efery man dat nefer vorks,
 Von frau should vranchised pe :
Dat ish de vay I solf dis ding,"
 Said Breitemann, said he.

Dey vented oop, dey vented down,
 'Tvas like a roarin' rifer,
De sighds vas here—de sighds vas dere—
 Und de vorldt vent on forefer.
" De more ve trinks, de more ve sees,
 Dis vorldt a derwisch pe ;
Das Werden's all von whirling droonk,"
 Said Breitemann, said he.

Schnitzerl's Philosopede.

PARDT FIRSDT.

Herr Schnitzerl make a philosopede,
    Von of de pullyest kind;
    It vent mitout a vheel in front,
And hadn't none pehind.
Von vheel vas in de mittel, dough,
    And it vent as sure as ecks,
For he shtraddled on de axle dree
    Mit de vheel petween his lecks.

Und ven he vant to shtart id off
    He paddlet mit his veet,
Und soon he cot to go so vast
    Dat avery dings he peat.
He run her out on Broader shtreed,
    He shkeeted like der vind,
Hei! how he bassed de vancy crabs,
    And lef dem all pehind!

De vellers mit de trottin nags
    Pooled oop to see him bass;
De Deutschers all erstaunished saidt:
    "*Potztausend! Was ist das?*"
Boot vaster shtill der Schnitzerl flewed
    On—mit a gashtly smile;

54

He tidn't tooch de dirt, py shings!
  Not vonce in half a mile.

Oh, vot ish all dis eartly pliss?
  Oh, vot ish man's soocksess?
Oh, vot ish various kinds of dings?
  Und vot ish hobbiness?
Ve find a pank-node in de shtreedt,
  Next dings der pank is preak;
Ve folls, und knocks our outsides in,
  Ven ve a ten shtrike make.

So vas it mit der Schnitzerlein
  On his philosopede.
His feet both shlipped outsideward shoost
  Vhen at his extra shpeed.
He felled oopon der vheel of course;
  De vheel like blitzen flew:
Und Schnitzerl he vas schnitz in vact
  For id sblished him grod in two.

Und as for his philosopede,
  Id cot so shkared, men say,
It pounded onward till it vent
  Ganz teufelwards afay.
Boot vhere ish now de Schnitzerl's soul?
  Vhere dos his shbirit pide?
In Himmel troo de entless pluc,
  It takes a medeor ride.

Schnitzerl's Philosopede.

PARDT SECONDT.

VEN Breitmann hear dat Schnitzerl
    Vas quardered into dwo,
  Und how his crate philosopede
To 'mi teufel had gone flew;
He dinked and dinked so heafy
    As only Deutschers can,
Denn saidt, "Who mighdt beliefet
    Dis ish de ent of man?

"De human souls of beoples
    Exisdt in deir ideés,
  Und dis of Wolfram Schnitzerl
    Mighdt dravel many vays,
In his *Bestimmung des Menschen*
    Der Fichte makes peliefe
Dat ve brogress oon-endly
    In vot pehind we leafe.

"De shbarrow falls ground-downwarts.
    Or drafels to de West;
De shbarrows dat coom afder
    Bild shoost de same oldt nest.
Man hat not vings or fedders,
    Und in oder dings, 'tis saidt,

He tont coom oop to shbarrows;
    Boot on nests he goes ahet.

"O vliest dou troo bornin vorldts
    Und nebuloser foam,
By monsdrous mitnight shiant forms
    Or vhere red tyfels roam,
Or vhere de chosts of shky rackets
    Peyond creadion flee?
Vhere'er dou art, oh Schnitzerlein!
    Crate saint! look down on me!

"Und deach me how you maket
    Dat crate philosopede,
Vitch roon dwice six mals vaster
    Ash any Arap shteed,
Und deach me how to 'stonish folk
    Und knock dem out de shpots.
Come pack to eart, O Schnitzerlein,
    Und pring it down to dots!"

Shoost ash dis vort vent outvarts
    Hans dinked he see a vlash,
Und unterwards de dable
    He doomple mit a crash,
Und to him, moong de glaesses,
    Und pottles ash vas proke,
Mit his het in a cigar box,
    An foice from Himmel shpoke:

"*Adsum Domine* Breitmann !
   Herr Capitain—here I pe !
So dell me right *honesté*
   Quare inquietasti me ?
Te video inter spoonibus,
   Et largis glassis too,
Cerevisia repletis,
   Sicut percussus tonitru !"

Denn Breitmann ansver Schnitzerl :
"*Coarctor nimis.*—See !
Siquidem Philistiim
   Pugnant adversum me.
Ergo vocavi te,
   Ash Saul *vocavit* Sam-
uel, *ut mi ostenderes*
   Quid teufel *faciam ?*"

Denn der shpirit, in Lateinisch
   Saidt "*Bene*—dat's de dalk !
Non habes in hoc shanty
   A shingle *et* some chalk ?
Non video inkum et calamos :
   (I shbose some bummer shdole 'em) :
Levate oculos tuos, son
   Et aspice ad linteolum !"

Den Breitmann see de chalk-piece
   Vitch riset from de floor,
Und signet a philosopede
   Alone oopon de toor,
De von dat Schnitzerl fabricate,
   Und oonderneat he see :
Probate inter equites :
   " Try dis in de cavallrie."

Den Breitmann shtoot ooprightly
   Und leanet on a bost,   [peen
Und saidt ; " If dis couldt, shouldt hafe
   It vouldt mighdt peen a chost !
Boot if it pe nouomenon,
   Phenomenoned indeed,
Or de soobyective obyectified,
   I'fe cot de philosopede."

Denn out he seekt a plack schmidt
   Ash vork in iron shteel ;
To make him a philosopede
   Mit shoost an only vheel.
De dings vas maket simple,
   Ash all crate ideés should pe ;
For 'twas noding boot a gart vheel
   Mit a two veet achsel-dree.

De dimes der Breitmann doomple
   In learnin for to ride,
Vas ofdener ash de sand grains
   Dat rollen in de tide.
De dimes he cot oopsetted
   In shdeerin lefdt und righdt,
Vas ofdener as de cleamin shdars
   Dat shtud de shky py nighdt.

Boot de vorstest of de veadures
   In dis von vheel horse, you bet,
Ish dat man couldt go so nicely
   Pefore he got oopset,
Some dimes he go like plazes
   Und toorn her, extra-fein,
Und denn shlop ofer—dis is vhat
   Hafe kill der Schnitzerlein.

Soosh droples as der Breitmann hafe
   To make dis 'vention go,
Vas nefer seen py mordal man
   Oopon dis vorldt pelow.
He doompled righdt, he doompled lefdt,
   He hafe a tousand toomps,
Dere nefer vas a gricket-ball
   Vot got soosh 'fernal boomps.

Boot ash he shvear't he'd do it,
　　He shvore id should pe done,
Dough he schimpft und fluchte laesterlich,
　　He visht he'd ne'er pegun.
Mit *Hagel! Blitz! Kreuzsakrament!*
　　He maket de houser ring,
Und hoped de Schnitzerl pe verdammt
　　For deachin him dis ding.

Nun—goot!　Ad last he got it.
　　Und peaudifool he goed,
Dis day, saidt he, "I'll stonish folk
　　A ridin on de road;
Dis day py shinks I'll do it!
　　Und knock dings out of sight!"
Ach weh! for Breitmann dat day
　　Vas not pe-markt mit vhite.

De noompers of de Deutsche folk
　　Dat coom dis feat to see,
I dink in soper earnest-hood,
　　Mighdt not ge-reckonet pe.
For miles dey shtood along de road,
　　Mein Gott! but dey vas dry;
Dey trinked den lager-beer shops oop,
　　Pefore der Hans coom py.

Vhen all at vonce drementous gries
  De fery country shook;
Und beoples shkreemt: "*Da ist er! Schau!*
  Dere ish der Breitmann!—Look!"
Mein Gott! vas efer soosh a shoudt?
  Vas efer soosh a gry?
Ven like a brick-bat in a vight,
  Der Breitemann roosh py.

O mordal man! Vy ish id, dow
  Hast passion to go vast?
Vy ish id dat de tog und horse
  Likes shbeed too quick to last?
De pugs, de pirds, de pumple-pees,
  Und all dat ish, 'twould seem,
Ish nefer hoppy boot, exsept
  When pilin on de shteam.

Der Breitmann flew! Von mighdy gry,
  Ash he vent scootin bast,
Von derriple, drementous yell—
  Dat day de virst—and last.
Vot ha! vot ho! Vy ish id dus?
  Vot makes dem shdare aghast?
Vy cooms dat vail of wild tespair?
  Ish somedings got gesmasht?

Yea—efen so. Yea, ferily—
  Shbeak, soul ! It is dy biz !
Der Breitmann shkeet so vast along,
  Dey fairly heard him whizz.
Ven shoost oopon a hill-top point
  It caught a pranch ge-pent,
Und like an opple vrom a svitch,
  Afay Hans Breitmann vent.

Vent troo de air a hoondert feet,
  (Allowin more or less)—
Denn *pobb—pobb—pobb*—a mile or dwo,
  He rollet along—I guess.
Say—hast dou seen a gannon ball
  Half shpent, shtill poundin on ;
Like made of gummi-lasticum ?
  So vent der Breitemann.

Dey bick him up—dey pring him in—
  No wort der Breitmann shpoke.
Der doktor look—he shvear erstaunt
  Dat nodings ish peen proke !
He rollet de rocky road entlong,
  He pouncet o'er shtock und shtone ?
You'd dink he'd knocked his outsides in,
  Yet nefer preak a pone !

All shtill Hans lay—bevilderfied—
   Nor seemet to mind de shaps,
Nor moofed, oontil der medicus
   Hafe dose him vell mit schnapps.
De schmell voke oop de boetry
   Of tays ven he vas young,
Und he murmulte de frogmends
   Of an sad romandic song:

"As summer pring de roses,
   Und roses pring de dew,
So Deutschland gifes de maidens
   Vot fetch de bier to you.
Komm Maidlein! Rothe Wænglein!
   Mit a wein glass in your paw!
Ve'll ged troonk amoong de roses
   Und lie soper on de shdraw!

"As winter prings de ice-wind,
   Dat plow o'er burg und hill,
Hard times pring in de lantlord,
   Und de lantlord pring de bill.
Boot sing Maidlein! Rothe Wængelein!
   Mit wein glass in your paw!
Ve'll ged troonk amoong de roses
   Und lie sober on de shdraw!"

Dey dook der Breitmann homewarts,
    Boot efer on de vay,
He nefer shbeaket no man,
    Und noding else could say:
Boot—"Maidlein—Rothe Wængelein!
    Mit wein glass in her paw,
We'll ged troonk amoong de rosen
    Und lie soper on de shdraw!"

Dey laid der Hans im Bette,
    Peneat de eider-doun,
Und sempled all de doktors
    Vot doktored in de town.
Dat ish, de Deutsche Aertzte,
    For Breitmann alfays says,
De Deutschers ish de onlies
    Mit originell idées.

Dere vas Doktor Moritz Schlinkenschlog,
    Dat vork ash caféopath,
Und der learned Cobus Schoepfskopf,
    Dat use de milchy bath;
Und Korschalitschky aus Boehmen,
    Vot cure mit slibovitz,
Und Wechselbalg from Berlin,
    Who only 'tend to fits.

Dere vas Strobbich aus Westfalen
  Who mofe all eart'ly ills
Mit concentrirter schinken juice,
  Und Pumpernickel pills;
Und a bier-kur man from Munich,
  Und a grape-curist from Rhein,
Und von who shkare tisease afay
  Mit dose of Schlesier wein.

So dey meed in consooldation
  Mit Doktor Winkeleck,
Who brackdise "renovation"
  Mit sauerkraut und speck.
Und dat no man shouldt pe shlightet
  Or treatet ash a tunce,
Dey 'greed to try deir systems
  Oopon Breitmann all at vonce.

Dat ish, mit de excepdion,
  Of gifin Schlesier wein;
For de remedy vas danger-full
  On von who trink from Rhine.
Ash der teufel once declaret
  Ven he taste it on a shpree,
Dat a man to trink soosh liquor
  Moost a born Silesian pe.

So de all vent los at Breitmann,
   Und woonderfool to dell,
He coomed to his gesundheit,
   Und pooty soon cot vell,
Some hinted at *Natura*
   Mit de oldt *vis sanatrix*,
Boot each dokter shvore *he* cured him,
   Und de rest were Taugenix.

I know not vot der Breitmann
   More newly has pegun,
Boot dey say he dalks day-daily
   Mit Dana of de *Sun*.
Dey dalk in Deutsch togeder,
   Und volk say de ent vill pe
Philosopedal changes
   In de Union cavallrie.

Gott help de howlin safage!
   Gott help de Indi-an!
Shouldt Breitmann choin his forces
   Mit Sheneral Sheridan.
Und denn to sing his braises
   Acain I'll gife a lied—
Hier hat dis dale an ende
   Of Breitmann's philosopede.

A Ballad apout de Rowdies.

De moon shines ofer de cloudlens,
    Und de cloudts plow ofer de sea,
    Und I vent to Coney Island,
  Und I took mein Schatz mit me.
Mine Schatz, Katrina Bauer,
    I gife her mein heart und vordt;
Boot ve tidn't know vot beoples
    De Dampsschiff hafe cot on poard.

De preeze plowed cool und bleasant,
    We looket at de town
Mit sonn-light on de shdeebles,
    Und wetter fanes doornin round.
Ve sat on de deck in a gorner
    Und dropled nopody dere,
Ven all aroundt oos de rowdies
    Peginned to plackguard und schvear!

A voman mit a papy
    Vas sittin in de blace;
Von tooket a chew tobacco
    Und trowed it indo her vace.
De voman got coonvulshons,
    De papy pegin to gry;
Und de rowdies shkreemed out a laffin,
    Und saidt dat de fun vas "high."

Pimepy ve become some hoonger
    Katrina Baur und I,
I openet de lit of mine pasket,
    Und pringed out a cherry bie.
A cherry kooken mit pretzels,
    "How goot!" Katrina said,
Ven a rowdy snatched it from her,
    Und preaked it ofer mine het.

I dells him he pe a plackguart
    I gifed him a biece my mind,
I vouldt saidt it pefore a tousand,
    Mit der teufel himself pehind.
Den he knocks me down mit a sloong-shot,
    Und peats me plack and plue ;
Und all de plackguards kick me,
    Dill I vainted, und dat ish drue.

De rich American beoples
    Don't know how de rowdies shtrike
Der poor hardt-workin Sherman,
    He knows it more ash he like.
If de Deutsche speakers und bapers
    Are sometimes too hard on dis land,
Shoost dink how de Deutsch kit driven
    Along by de rowdy's hand !

Wein Geist.

I STOOMPLED oud ov a dafern,
    Berauscht mit a gallon of wein,
Und I rooshed along de Strassen,
    Like a derriple Eberschwein.

Und like a lordly boar-big,
    I doompled de soper folk;
Und I trowed a shtone droo a shdreed lamp,
    Und bot' of de classes I proke.

Und a gal vent roonin' bast me.
    Like a vild coose on de vings,
Boot I gatch her for all her skreechin,
    Und giss her like afery dings.

Und denn mit an board und a shdore-box.
    I blay de horse-viddle a biece,
Dill de neighbours shkreem "deat'!" und
        "murder!"
    Und holler aloudt "bolice?"

Und vhen der crim night wæchter
    Says all of dis foon moost shtop,
I oop mit mein oombrella,
    Und schlog him ober de kop.

I leaf him like tead on de bavemend,
　　Und roosh droo a darklin' lane.
Dill moonlighd und tisdand musik,
　　Pring me roundt to my soul again.

Und I sits all oonder de linden,
　　De hearts-leaf linden dree;
Und I dink of de quick ge-vanisht lofe
　　Dat vent like de vind from me.
Und I voonders in mine dipsy hood.
　　If a damsel or dream vas she!

Dis life ish all a lindens
　. Mit holes dat show de Plue;
Und pedween de finite pranches,
　　Cooms Himmel light shinin troo.

De blaetter are raushlin' o'er me,
　　Und efery leaf ish a fay,
Und dey vait dill de Windsbraut comet.
　　To pear dem in Fall afay.

Und I look at a rock py de rifer,
　　Vhere a stein ish of harpe form,
—Year dausend in, oud, it shtandet—
　　Und nopody blays but de shtorm.

Here vonce on a dimes a vitches,
　Soom melodies here peginned,
De harpe ward all zu steine,
　Die melodie ward zu wind.

Und so mit dis tox-i-cation,
　Vitch hardens de outer Me;
Uber stein and schwein, de weine,
　Shdill harps oud a melodie.

Boot deeper de Ur-lied ringet,
　Ober stein und wein und svines,
Dill it endet vhere all peginnet,
　Und alles wird ewig zu eins,
In de dipsy, treamless sloomper
　Vhich units de Nichts und Seyns.

Breitmann in Politics.

I.—The Nomination.

WHEN ash de var vas ober,
    Und Beace her shnow-wice vings,
    Vas vafin o'er de coondry
(In shpods) like afery dings;
Und heroes vere revardtet,
    De beople all pegan
To say 'tvas shame dat nodings
    Vas done for Breitemann.

No man wised how id vas shtartet,
    Or where der fore shlog came,
Boot dey shveared it vas a cinder,
    Dereto a purnin shame :
" Dere is Schnitzerl in de Gustom-House—
    Potzblitz ! can dis dings pe ?—
Und Breitmann he hafe nodings :
    Vot sights is dis to see !

" Nod de virst ret cendt for Breitmann !
    Ish *dis* do pe de gry
On de man dat sacked de repels
    Und trinked dem high und dry ?

By meine Seel' I shvears id,
  Und vot's more I deglares id's drue,
He vonce gleaned out a down in half an oor,
  Und shtripped id strumpf und shoe.

" He was shoost like Kœnig Etzel,
    Of whom de shdory dell,
  Der Hun who go for de Romans
    Und gife dem shinin hell,
  Only dis dat dey say no grass vouldt crow
    Vhere Etzel's horse had trot,
  Und I really peliefe vere Breitmann go
    De hops shpring oop, bei Gott!"

If once you tie a dog loose,
  Dere ish more soon gets arount,
Und wenn dis vas shtartedt on Breitmann
  It was rings aroom be-foundt;
Dough *vhy* he *moost* hafe somedings
  Vas not by no mean glear,
Nor tid id, like Paulus' confersion,
  On de snap to all abbear!

Und, in facdt, Balthazar Bumchen
  Saidt he couldtent nicht blainly see
Vy a veller for gadderin riches
  Shood dus revartedt pe :
10

Der Breitmann own drei Houser,
   Mit a wein-handle in a stohr,
Dazu ein Lager-Wirthschaft,
   Und sonst was—somedings more

Dis plasted plackguard none-sense
   Ve couldn't no means shtand,
From a narrow-mineted shvine's kopf,
   Of our nople captain grand :
Soosh low, goarse, betty *bornirtheit*
   A shentleman deplores ;
So ve called him *verfluchter Hundsfott*
   Und shmysed him out of toors.

So ve all dissolfed dat Breitmann
   Shouldt hafe a nomination
To go to de Legisladoor,
   To make some dings off de nation ;
Mit de helb of a Connedigut man,
   In whom ve hafe great hobes,
Who hat shange his boledics fivdeen dimes,
   Und derefore knew de robes.

II.—The Committee of Instruction.

OENN for our Insdructions Comedy
    De ding vas protocollirt,
By Docktor Emsig Grubler,
    Who in Jena vonce studiret;
Und for Breitmann his instrugtions
    De Comedy tid say
Dat de All out-going from de Ones
    Vash die first Moral Idée.

Und de segondt crate Moral Idée
    Dat into him ve rings,
Vas dat government for avery man
    Moost alfays do avery dings;
Und die next Idée do vitch his mindt
    Esbecially ve gall,
Ish to do mitout a Bresident
    Und no government at all.

Und die fourt Idée ve vish der Hans
    Vouldt alfays keeb in fiew,
Ish to cooldifate die Peaudifool,
    Likewise de Goot and Drue;
Und de form of dis oopright-hood
    In proctise to present,
He most get our little pills all bassed
    Mitout id's gostin a cent.

Und die fift' Idée—ash learnin
   Ish de cratest ding on cart,
And ash Shoopider der Vater
   To Minerfa gife ge-birt'—
Ve peg dat Breitmann oonto oos
   All pooblic tockuments
Vich he can grap or shteal vill sendt—
   Franked—mit his gompliments.

Die sechste crate Moral Idée—
   Since id fery vell ish known
Dat mind ish de resooldt of food,
   Ash der Moleschott has shown,
Und ash mind ish de highest form of Gott
   As in Fichte dot' abbear—
He moost alfays go mit de barty
   Dat go for lager-bier.

Now ash all dese instrugdions
   Vere showed to Misder Twine,
De Yangee boledician,
   He say dey vere fery fine:
Dey vere pesser ash goot, und almosdt nice—
   A tarnal tall concern ;—
Boot dey hafe some little trawpacks,
   Und in fagdt weren't worth a dern.

Boot yed, mit our bermission,
    If de shentlemans allow—
Here all der Shermans in de room
    Dake off deir hats und pow—
He vouldt gife our honored gandidate
    Some nodions of his own,
Hafing managed some elecdions
    Mit sookcess, as vell vas known.

Let him plow id all his *own* vay,
    He'd pet as sure as born,
Dat our mann vouldt not coom out of
    Der liddle endt der horn,
Mit his goot *proad* Sherman shoulders—
    Dis maket oos laugh, py shink!
So de comedy shtart for Breitmann's—
    Nota bene—afder a trink!

III.—Mr. Twine Explains Being "Scund Upon the Goose."

OERE in his crate corved oaken shtuhl
    Der Breitmann sot he:
He lookt shoost like de shiant
    In de Kinder hishdorie;
Und pefore him, on de tische,
    Vas—vhere man alfays foundt it—
Dwelf inches of goot lage.,
    Mit a Bœmisch glass aroundt it.

De foorst vordt dat der Breitmann spoke.
    He maked no sbeech or sign:
De next remark vas, "*Zapfet aus!*"—
    De dird vas, "*Schenket ein!*"
Vhen in coomed liddle Gottlieb
    Und Trina mit a shtock
Of allerbest Markgraefler wein—
    Dazu dwelf glaeser Bock.

Denn Misder Twine deglare dat he
    Vas happy to denounce
Dat as Copdain Breitmann suited oos
    Egsockdly do an ounce,

He vas ged de nomination,
    And need nod more eckshblain:
Der Breitmann dink in silence,
    And denn roar aloudt, CHAMPAGNE!

Den Mishder Twine, while trinken wein,
    Mitwhiles vent on do say,
Dat long insdruckdions in dis age
    Vere nod de dime of tay;
Und de only ding der Breitmann need
    To pe of any use
Vas shoost to dell to afery mans
    He's *soundt oopon der coose.*

Und ash dis little frase berhops
    Vas nod do oos bekannt,
He dakes de liberdy do make
    Dat ve shall oondershtand,
And vouldt tell a liddle shdory
    Vitch dook blace pefore de wars:
Here der Breitmann nod to Trina,
    Und she bass aroundt cigars.

"Id ish a longe dime, now here,
    In Bennsylvanien's Shtate,
All in der down of Horrisburg
    Dere rosed a vierce depate,

'Tween vamilies mit cooses,
  Und dose vhere none vere foundt—
If cooses might, by common law,
  Go squanderin aroundt?

"Dose who vere nod pe-gifted
  Mit gooses, und vere poor,
All shvear de law forbid dis crime,
  Py shings and cerdain sure;
But de coose-holders teklare a coose
  Greadt liberty tid need,
And to pen dem oop vas gruel,
  Und a mosdt oon-Christian teed.

"Und denn anoder party
  Idself tid soon refeal,
Of arisdograts who kepd no coose,
  Pecause 'twas not shendeel:
Tey tid not vish de splodderin geese
  Shouldt on deir pafemends bass,
So dey shoined de anti-coosers,
  Or de oonder lower glass!"

Here Breitmann led his shdeam out:
  "Dis shdory goes to show
Dat in poledicks, ash lager,
  Virtus in medio.

De drecks ish ad de pottom—
  De skoom floads high inteed;
Boot das bier ish in de mittle,
  Says an goot old Sherman lied.

" Und shoost apout elegdion-dimes
  De scoom und drecks, ve see,
Have a pully Wahl-verwandtschaft,
  Or election-sympathie."
" Dis is very vine," says Misder Twine,
  " Vot here you indroduce:
Mit your bermission, I'll grack on
  Mit my shdory of de coose.

" A gandertate for sheriff
  De coose-beholders run,
Who shvear de coose de noblest dings
  Vot valk peneat de sun;
For de cooses safe de Capidol
  In Rome long dimes ago,
Und Horrisburg need safin
  Mighty pad, ash all do know.

" Acainsd dis mighdy Goose-man
  Anoder veller rose,
Who keepedt himself ungommon shtill
  Ven oders came to plows;

Und if any ask how 'twas he shtoodt,
His vriends wouldt vink so loose,
Und visper ash dey dapped deir nose :
'*He's soundt oopon de coose!*

" ' He's O. K. oopon de soobject ;
 Shoost pet your pile on dat ;
On dis bartik'ler quesdion
 He intends to coot it fat.'
So de veller cot elegded
 Pefore de beople foundt
On *vitch* site of der coose it vas
 He shtick so awful soundt.

" Dis shdory's all I hafe to dell,"
 Says Misder Hiram Twine ;
" Und I advise Herr Breitmann
 Shoost to vight id on dis line."
De volk who of dese boledics
 Would oder shapters read,
Moost waiten for de segondt pardt
 Of dis here Breitmann's Lied.

IV.—How Breitmann and Schmit were Reported to be Log-Rolling.

ID happenet in de yar of crace,
   Ven all dese dings pegan,
Dat Mishder Schmit, de shap who rooned
Acainsd der Breitemann,
   Vas a man who look like Mishder Twine
So moosh dat beoples say
   Dey pliefe dey moost ge-brudert pe—
Gott weiss in vot a vay!

Und id vas also moosh be-marked—
   Vitch look shoost like a bruder—
Dat ven Twine vas vork on any side
   Der Schmit vas on de oder:
A fery gommon dodge ish dis
   Mit de arisdocracie;
So dat votefer cardt toorns oop,
   Id's game for de familie!

Nun, goot! Howefer dis mighdt pe,
   'Tvas cerdain on dis hit
Der Twine vas do his teufelest
   To euchre Mishder Schmit;
Und Schmit, I criefe to say, exglaimed:
   "Goll darn me for a fool,
But I'll smash old Dutch to cholera fits
   And rake the eternal pool!"

So dey cot some liddle ledders,
    Ash brifate ash could pe,
Vitch Breitmann writed long agone
    To friendts in Germany;
Und dey brinted dem in efery vay
    To make de beoples laugh,
Und comment on dem in de shtyle
    Dat "sports" call "slasher-gaff."

Dere to—as vash known py shoodshment
    Und glearly ascerdaind,
Dat Breitmann hafe lossed money
    Py a valse und schwindlin friend—
So dey roon it troo de newsbapers,
    Und shbeech do make pegan,
Dat *Breitmann* shtole de gelt himself
    Und rop der oder man.

Boot de ding dat jam de hardest
    On de men dat bull de vires,
Und showed dat Captain Breitmann
    Shtood pedween dwo heafy vires,
Vas, pecause he vas a soldier—
    Von could see id at a clanse—
Dey had pud him in a tisdrigt
    Vhere he hadn't half a shanse.

For ash de pold solidaten
  Ish more prafe ash oder mans,
Dey moost lead de hope verloren
  Und pattle in de vans;
Und ash defeat ish honoraple
  To men in honor shtrict,
Dey honor dem py puttin em
  Vhere dey're cerdain to pe licked.

Boot dis dimes it shlopped over,
  Tvas de dird or secondt heat
Dat a soldier in dis tisdrigt
  Had been poot oop und beat:
So de Plue Goats dink it over
  Und go quietly to vork:
De bow ven too moosh aufgespannt
  Vlies packward mit a yerk.

Now Mishder Twine deglaret on dis
  De ding seemed doubtenfull,
Boot mitout delay he dook de horns
  So poldly py de bull,
Und shpread de shdory eferyvhere,
  Dill folk to pliefe pegan,
Dat Mishder Schmit had *sold de vight*
  Unto der Breitemann!

He fix de liddle tedails—
 How moosh der Schmit hafe got
For sellin out his barty
 To let Breitmann haul de pot;
Und he showed a brifate ledder
 From Breitemann to Schmit,
Vhere he bromise him for Congress
 If he shoost let oop a bit.

Der Twine vas writet dis ledder;
 For der Copitain Breitemann
Vould nefer hafe shtood soosh hoompoogks
 Since virst his life pegan;
He hat tone some rough dings in der war,
 In de ploonder-und-morder line,
Boot vas hoockelperry-persimmoned
 Mit dese boledics of Twine.

Howefer, dis ledder vorket foorst-rade—
 Mit de Merigans pest of all,
For dey mostly dinked it de naturalest ding
 As efer couldt pefall;
For to sheat von's own gonstituents
 Ish de pest mofe in de came,
Und dey nefer sooposed a Dootchman
 Hafe de sense to do de same

V.—How they held the Mass Meeting.

DERE's nodings in dis vorldt so pad,
    Ash all oov us may learn,
    Boot may shange from dark to lighthood,
If loock should dake a doorn ;
So it happenet mit Breitmann,
    Who in shpite of sin und Schmit,
Gontrified ad shoost dis yooncture
    Do make a glucky hit.

Dey hat sendet out some plackarts
    To de Deutsche buergers all
(N. B.—Dish ish not mean *plackarts*,
    Boot de pills dey shtick on de vall),
To say dat a Massenversammlung—
    Or a meeding of all de masses—
Vould be held in de Arbeiter-Halle,
    To consisd of de Sharman classes.

Now dey gife de brintin of de pills
    To a new gekommene man,
Who dinked dat Demokratisch
    Vas de same ash Repooblican :
Gott in Himmel weiss where he hid himself
    On dish free Coloompian shore
Dat he scaped de naturalizationisds,
    Und hadn't found out pefore.

Boot to dis Deutsche brinter,
  De only tifference he
Petween Repooblicanish
  Und Demokratisch tid see,
Vas dat von vash dwo ledders longer;
  So he dook shoost vot seem pat
To make de poster handsome—
  Likewise a liddle fat.

How ofden in dis buzzlin life
  Small grubs grows oop to vings!
How ofden shoost from moostard seet
  A virst-glass pusiness shprings!
Vant klein komt men tot't groote,
  Ash de Hollanders hafe said :
Mit dese dwo ledders Breitemann
  Caved in der Schmitsy's head.

VI.—Breitmann's Great Speech.

Dis tale dat Schmit hafe *sett de right*
    Cot so much put apout
Dat many of his beoples vere
    In fery tupious toubt;
'Pove all, dose who were on de make,
    And easy change deir lodge,
Und, pein awfool smart demselfs,
    Pelieve in every dodge.

Vhen de meeding vas gesempled,
    Und dey found no Schmit vas dere,
Dey looket at von anoder
    Mit a *ganz* erstaunished air;
But dey *saw it* glear as taylight,
    Und around a vink dere ran,
Ven pefore dem rose de shiant form
    Of Copitain Breitemann!

Den Breitemann vent los at dem:
    "He could nichts well exbress
De rapdure dat besqueezed his hearts—
    De wonnevol hoppiness—
To meed in friendlich council
    And glasp de hand of dose
Who had peen mit most oonreason
    Und unkindtly galled his foes.

"Berhaps o'er all dis shmilin cart'—
   He vould say it dere and den—
Soosh shpecdagles couldt nod pe seen
   Of soosh imbartial men,
So tefoid of pase sospicion,
   So apove all betty dricks,
Ash to gome und lisden vairly
   To a voe in poledicks;

"Dat ish to say, a so-galled voc—
   For he feeled id in his soul
Dat de *brinciples* vitch mofed dem
   Vere de same oopon de whole;
But he lack a vord to exbress dem
   In manners opportunes—"
Here a veller in de gallery
   Gry oud, oonkindly, "Shpoons!"

Und dere der Breitmann goppled him:
   "If *shpoons* our modifes pe,
Dere's not a man pefore oos
   Who lossed a shpoon by me:
Far rader had I gife you all
   A shpoons to eaten mit,
Und I hope to get a ladle for
   Mine friendt, der Mishder Schmit."

Dis fetch das Haus like doonder—
    It raised der teufel's dust,
Und for sefen-lefen minudes
    Dey ooplauded on a bust;
Und de blokes dat dinked of hedgin
    Saw a ring as round as O;
So dey boked cash oder in de rips,
    Und said, "I dold you so!"

For dis d'lusion to de ladle
    Vas as glear ash city milk,
Und drawd it on de beoples
    So vine ash flossen silk,
Dat Hans und Schmit vere rollin locks,
    Und de locks were ready cut;
Only Breitmann hafe de liddle end,
    Und Schmitsy dake de butt!

Den Breitemann he crack onward:
    "If any 'lightened man
Will seeken in his Bibel,
    He'll find dat a publican
Is a barty ash sells lager;
    Und das ding is ferry blain,
Dat a *re*-publican ish von
    Who sells id 'gain und 'gain.

"Now since dat I sells lager,
    I gant agreen mit
De demprance brinciples I hear
    Distriputet to Schmit;
Boot dis I dells you vairly,
    Und no one to teseife—
If I were Schmit, I'd pliefen
    Shoost vot der Schmit peliefe.

"And to mine Sherman, liperal friends
    I might mention in dis shpot
Dat I hear an oonfoundet rumor
    Dat der Schmit peliefe in Gott;
Und also dat he coes to shoorsh—
    Mit a prayer-book for salfadion:
I vould not for die welt say dings
    To hoort his repudadion.

"Und nodin is more likely
    Dat it all a shlander pe,
So also de rumor dat ven young
    He shtoody divinidy:
I myself, ash a publican,
    Moost pe a sinner by fate,
Und in dis sense I denounce myself
    Ash Re-publi-candidate!

" Und dat ve may meed in gommon,
 I declare here in dis hall—
Und I shvears mineself to hold to it,
 Fotefer may pefall—
Dat any man who gifes me his fote—
 Votevefer his boledicks pe—
Shall alfays pe regartet
 Ash bolidigal friendt py me."

(Dis voonderfol condescension
 Pring down drementous applause,
Und dose who catch de nodion
 Gife most derriple hooraws;
Eshbecially some Amerigans
 Ash vas shtandin near de door,
Und who in all deir leben long
 Nefer heard so moosh sense pefore.)

" Dese ish de brincibles I holts,
 And dose in vitch I run :
Dey ish fixed firm and immutaple
 Ash te course of de 'ternal sun :
Boot if you ton't abbrove of dem—
 Blease nodice vot I say—
I shall only pe too happy
 To alder dem right afay.

" Und unto my Demogratic friendts
   I vould very glearly shtate—
Since dis useless mit oop-geclearéd minds
   To hold a long depate—
Dat dere's no man in de cidy
   Dat sells besser liquor ash I,
Und I shtand de treadts *free-gradis*
   Vhenefer mine friendts ish try.

" *Ad finem*—in de ende—
   I moost mendion do you all,
Dat a dootzen parrels of lager bier
   Ish a-gomin to dis hall:
Dere ish none of mine own barty here,
   Boot we'll do mitout deir helfs;
Und I kess, on de whole, 'twill pe shoost so goot.
   If ve trink it all ourselfs."

Soosh drementous up-loudation
   Pefore was nefer seen,
Ash dey shvored dat Copitan Breitmann
   Vas a brick-pat, and no sardine;
Und dey trinked demselfs besoffen,
   Sayin, " Hope you wird sookceed !"—
De nexter theil will pe de ent
   Of dis historisch lied.

VII.—The Author Asserts the Vast Intellectual Superiority of Germans to Americans.

Dere's a liddle fact in hishdory
　　Vich few hafe oonderstand—
Dat de Deutschers are, *de jure*,
　　De owners of dis land;
Und I brides mineself unspeakbarly
　　Dat I foorst make be-known
De primordial cause dat Colupmus
　　Vas derivet from Cologne;

For ash his name vas Colon,
　　It fisibly does shine
Dat his elders are geboren been
　　In Co-logne on der Rhein;
Und Colonia pein a colony,
　　It sehr bemarkbar ist
Dat Columbus in America
　　Was der firster colonist.

Und ash Columbus is a tofe,
　　Id is wort de drople to mark
Dat a bidgeon foorst tiscofered land
　　A-vlyin from de ark;
Und shtill wider—in de peginnin,
　　Mitout de leastest toubt,
A tofe vas vly ofer de wassers
　　Und pring de vorldt herout.

Ash mine goot oldt teacher der Kreutzer
    To me tid often shbeak,
De mythus of name rebeats idself
    (Vich ve see in his *Symbolik*);
So also de name America,
    If ve a liddle look,
Vas coom from de oldt King Emerich
    In de Deutsche *Heldenbuch*.

Und id vas from dat very *Heldenbuch*—
    How voonderful id run!—
Dat I shdole de "Song of Hildebrand,
    Or der Vater und der Son,"
Und dishtripute it to Breitmann,
    For a reason vitch now ish plain,
Dat dis Sagen-Cyclus, full-endet,
    Pring me round to der Hans again!

Dese laws of un-endly un-wigglin
    Ish so teep und broad und tall
Dat nopody boot a Deutscher
    Have a het to versteh dem at all;
Und should I write mine dinks all oud,
    I ton't peliefe, indeed,
Dat I mineself vould versteh de half
    Of dis here Breitmannslied.

Ash de Hegel say of his system,
    Dat only von mans knew
Vot der teufel id meandt, und *he* could't tell;
    Und der Jean Paul Richter too,
Who said, " Gott knows I meant somedings
    When foorst dis buch I writ,
Boot Gott only wise vot de buch means now,
    Vor I have vergotten it."

And all of dis be-wises
    So blain ash de face on your nose,
Dat der Deutscher hafe efen more intellects,
    Dan he himself soopose;
Und his tifference mit de over-again vorldt,
    Ash I really do soospect,
Ish dat oder volk hafe more *soopose*,
    Und lesser intellect.

Yet ooprightly I gonfess it—
    Mitout ashkin vhy or vhence—
Dere ish also dimes vhen Amerigans
    Hafe ge-shown sharp-pointed sense;
Und a fery outsigned example
    Of genius in dis line
Vas dishblayed in dis elegdion
    Py Mishder Hiram Twine.

VIII.—Showing How Mr. Hiram Twine "Played off" on Smith.

VIDE LICET: Dere vas a fillage
    Whose vode alone vouldt pe
    Apout enoof to elegdt a man,
  Und gife a mayority;
So de von who couldt scoop dis seddlement
    Vould make a pully hit;
Boot dough dey vere Deutschers, von und all,
    Dey all go von on Schmit.

Now it happenet to gome to bass
    Dat in dis liddle town
De Deutsch vas all exshpegdin
    Dat Mishder Schmit coom down,
His brinciples to fore-setzen
    Und his ideés to deach,
(Dat is, fix oop de brifate pargains)
    Und telifer a pooblic sbeech.

Now Twine vas a gyrotwistive cuss,
    Ash blainly ish peen shown,
Und vas alfays an out-findin
    Votefer might pe known;
Und mit some of his circums windles
    He fix de matter so
Dat he'd pe himself at dis meetin
    And see how dings vas go.

Oh shtrangely in dis leben
   De dings kits vorked apout!
Oh voonderly Fortuna
   Makes toorn us insite out!
Oh sinkular de luck-wheel rolls!
   Dis liddle meeding dere
Fixt Twine *ad perpendiculum*—
   Shoost suit him to a hair!

Now it hoppenit on dis efenin
   De Deutschers, von und all,
Vere avaitin mit impatience
   De openin of de ball;
Und de shates of nite vere fallin
   Und de shdars begin to plink,
Und dey vish dat Schmit vouldt hoorry,
   For d'vas dime to dake a trink.

Dey hear some hoofs a-dramplin,
   Und dey saw, und dinked dey knowed,
Der bretty greature coomin,
   On his horse along de road;
Und ash he ride town in-ward,
   De likeness vas so plain
Dey donnered out, "Hooray for Schmit!"
   Enough to make it rain.

Der Twine vas shtart like plazes;
  Boot oopshtarted too his wit,
Und he dinks, " Great Turnips ! what if I
  Could bass for Colonel Schmit?
Gaul dern my heels ! *I'll do it,*
  Und go the total swine !
Oh, Soap-balls ! what a chance !" said dis
  Dissembulatin Twine.

Den 'twas " Willkomm ! willkomm, Mishder
  Schmit !"
  Ringsroom on efery site ;
Und " First-rate ! How dy-do yourself?"
  Der Hiram Twine replied.
Dey ashk him, " Come und dake a trink ?"
  But dey find it mighdy queer
Ven Twine informs dem none boot hogs
  Vould trink dat shtinkin bier ;

Dat all lager vas nodings boot boison ;
  Und ash for Sherman wein,
He dinks it vas erfounden
  Exshbressly for Sherman schwein ;
Dat he himself vas a demperanceler—
  Dat he gloria in de name ;
Und atfise dem all, for tecency's sake,
  To go und do de same.

Dese bemarks among de Deutschers
  Vere apout ash vell receife
Ash a cats in a game of den-bins,
  Ash you may of coorse peliefe:
De heat of de reception
  Vent down a dootzen tegrees,
Und in place of hurraws dere vas only heardt
  De rooslin of de drees.

Und so in solemn stille
  Dey scorched him to de hall,
Vhere he maket de oradion
  Vitch vas so moosh to blease dem all;
Und dis vay he pegin it:
  " Pefore I furder go,
I vish dat my obinions
  You puddin-het Dootch should know.

"Und ere I norate to you,
  I think it only fair
We should oonderstand each other
  Prezactly, chunk and square.
Dere are boints on vhich ve tisagree,
  And I will plank de facts—
I don't go round slanganderin
  My friendts pehind deir packs.

" So I beg you dake it easy
   If on de raw I touch,
Vhen I say I can't apide de sound
   Of your groontin, shi-shing Dutch.
Should I in the Legisladure
   As your slumgullion shtand,
I'll have a bill forbidding Dutch
   Troo all dis 'versal land.

"Should a husband talk it to his frau,
   To deat' he should pe led;
If a mutter breat' it to her shild,
   I'd bunch her in de head;
Und I'm sure dat none vill atfocate
   Ids use in public schools,
Oonless dey're peastly, nashdy, prutal,
   Sauerkraut-eatin vools.

Here Mishder Twine, to gadder breat,
   Shoost make a liddle pause,
Und see sechs hundert gapin eyes,
   Sechs hundert shdarin chaws,
Dey shtanden erstarrt like frozen;
   Von faindly dried to hiss;
Und von set: " Ish it shleeps I'm treamin?
   Gottausend! vat ish dis?"

Twine keptet von eye on de vindow,
    Boot poldly went ahet:
"Of your oder shtinkin hobits·
    No vordt needt hier pe set.
Shtop goozlin bier—shtop shmokin bipes—
    Shtop rootin in de mire;
Und shoost *un-Dutchify* yourselfs:
    Dat's all dat I require."

Und *denn* dere coomed a shindy
    Ash if de shky hat trop:
"Trow him mit ecks, py doonder!
    Go shlog him on de kop!
Hei! Shoot him mit a powie-knifes;
    Go for him, ganz and gar!
Shoost tar him mit some fedders!
    Led's fedder him mit tar!"

Sooch a teufel's row of furie
    Vas nefer oop-kickt before:
Soom roosh to on-climb de blatform—
    Soom hoory to fasten te toor:
Von veller vired his refolfer,
    Boot de pullet missed her mark:
She coot de cort of de shandelier:
    It vell, und de hall vas tark!

Oh vell was it for Hiram Twine
   Dat nimply he couldt shoomp;
Und vell dat he light on a misthauf,
   Und nefer feel de boomp;
Und vell for him dat his goot cray horse
   Shtood sattled shoost outside;
Und vell dat in an augenblick
   He vas off on a teufel's ride.

Bang! bang! de sharp pistolen shots
   Vent pipin py his ear,
Boot he tortled oop de barrick road
   Like any mountain deer:
Dey trowed der Hiram Twine mit shteins,
   But dey only could be-mark
Von climpse of his vhite obercoadt,
   Und a clotterin in de tark.

So dey all versembled togeder,
   Ein ander to sprechen mit,
Und allow dat sooch a rede
   Dey nefer exshpegd from Schmit—
Dat he vas a foorst-glass plackguard,
   And so pig a Lump ash ran;
So, *nemine contradicente,*
   Dey vented for Breitemann.

Und 'twas annerthalb yar dereafter
    Before der Schmit vas know
Vot maket dis rural fillage
    Go pack oopon him so;
Und he schvored at de Dootch more schlimmer
    Ash Hiram Twine had tone.
Nota bene: He tid it in earnesht,
    Vhile der Hiram's vas pusiness fun.

Boot vhen Breitmann heard de shdory
    How de fillage hat peen dricked,
He shvore bei Leib und Leben
    He'd rader hafe been licked
Dan pe helpet bei soosh shumgoozlin;
    Und 'twas petter to pe a schwein
Dan a schwindlin honeyfooglin shnake,
    Like dat lyin Yankee Twine.

Und pegot so heafy disgoosted
    Mit de boledicks of dis land
Dat his friendts couldn't barely keep him
    From trowin oop his hand,   [poot;
Vhen he helt shtraidt flush, mit an ace in his
    Vich phrase ish all de same,
In de science of de pokerology,
    Ash if he got de game.

So Breitmann cot elegtet,
  Py vollowin de vay
Dey manage de elegdions
  Unto dis fery day;
Vitch shows de Deutsch *Dummehrlichkeit*,
  Also de Yankee " wit:"
Das ist das Abenteuer
  How Breitmann lick der Schmit

Breitmann's Going to Church.

"*Vides igitur, Collega carissime, visitationem canonicam esse rem haud ita periculosam, sed valde amœnam, si modo vinum, groggio, et cibi praesto sunt.*"
[*Novissimæ Epistolæ Obscurorum Virorum. Berlini, F. Berggold*, 1869. *Epistola* xxiii. *p.* 63.]

'vas near de State of Nashfille,
   In de town of Tennessee,
    Der Breitmann vonce vas quarderd
  Mit all his cavallrie.
Der Sheneral kept him glose in camp,
  He vouldn't let dem go,
Dey couldn't shdeal de first plack hen,
  Or make de red cock crow.

Und virst der Breitmann vildly shmiled,
  Und denn he madly shvore:
"Crate h—l mit shpoons und shinsherbread!
  Can dis pe makin war?
Verdammt pe all der discipline;
  Verdammt der Shenerál;
Vere I vonce on de road, his will
  Were Wurst mir und egâl.

"Oh vhere ish all de plazin roofs
    Dat claddened vonce mine eyes,
Und vhere de crand blantaschions
    Vhere ve gaddered many a brize?
Und vhere de plasted shpies ve hung
    A howlin loud mit fear;
Und vhere de rascal push-whackers
    Ve shashed like vritened deer.

"De roofs are shtandin fast und firm
    Mit repels blottin oonder;
De crand blantaschions lie round loose
    For Morgan's men to ploonder;
De shbies go valkin out und in,
    Ash sassy ash can pe,
Und in de voods de push-whackers
    Are makin foon of me!

"O, vere I on my schimmel grey,
    Mein sabre in mein hand,
Dey should drack me py de ruins
    Of de houses troo de land.
Dey should drack me py de puzzards
    High sailen ofer head,
A vollowin der Breitmann's trail,
    To claw de repel dead."

Outspoke der bold Von Stossenheim,
  Who had théories of Gott:
"O Breitmann dis ish shoodgement on
  De vays dat you hafe trot
You only lifes to joy yourself,
  Yet you yourself moost say
Dat self-development requires
  De réligiös Idée."

Dey set dem down und argued it,
  Like Deutschers vree from fear,
Dill dey schmoke ten pfounds of Knaster
  Und drinked drei fass of bier.
Der Breitmann go py Schopenhauer,
  Boot Veit he had him denn,
For he dook him on de angles
  Of de moral oxygen.

Der Breitmann 'low dat 'pentence
  Ish known in afery glime,
Und dat to grin und bear it
  Vas healty und sooplime.
"For mine Sout Sherman Catoliks
  Id vas pe goot I know,
Likevise dem Nordland Luterans,
  If vonce to shoorsh dey go.

"Boot how vas id mit oders
  Who dinks philosophic?
I don't begreif de matter—"
    Said Stossenheim: "Denn see
De more dat Shoorsh disgoostet you,
  Und make despise und bain,
De crater merid ish to go,
  Und de crater ish your gain.

"I know a liddle shoorsh mineself
    Oopon de Bole Jack road;
  (De rebs vonce shot dree Federals dere
    Ash into shoorsh dey goed.)
Dere you might make a bilerimage,
    Und do it in a tay:—
Gott only knows vot dings you might
    Bick oop, oopon de vay."

Den oop dere shpoke a contrapand,
    Vas at de tent id's toor:
"Dere's twenty bar'ls of whisky hid
    In dat tabernacle—shore!
A rebel he done gone and put
    It in de cellar true;
No libin man dat secret knows
    'Cept only me an' you."

Der Stossenheim he grossed himself
   Und knelt peside de fence,
Und gried: "O Coptain Breitmann, see,
   Die finger Providence."
Der Breitmann droed his hat afay:
   Says he, "Pe't hit or miss,
I'fe heard of miragles pefore,
   Boot none so hunk ash dis.

"Wohl auf, mine pully cafaliers,
   Ve'll ride to shoorsh to-day!
Each man ash hasn't cot a horse,
   Moost shteal von, rite afay.
Dere's a raw, green corps from Michigan,
   Mit horses on de loose;
You men ash vants some hoof-iróns,
   Look out und crip deir shoes!"

All brooshed und fixed, de cavallrie
   Rode out py moonen-shine;
De cotten fields in shimmerin light
   Lay white ash elfenbein.
Dey heared a shot close py Lavergne,
   Und men who rode afay.
In de road a-velterin in his ploot
   A Federal picket lay.

Und all dat he hafe dimes to say:
  "Vhile shtandin at my post,
De guerillas got first shot at me;"
  Und so gafe oop de ghost.
Den a contrapand, who helt his head,
  Said: "Sah—dose grillers all,
Is only half a mile from hyar,
  A dancin at a pall."

Der Breitmann shpoke, und brummed it out
  Ash if his heart tid schvell,
"I'll gife dem music at dat pall
  Vill tantz dem indo hell!"
Hei!—arrow-fast—a teufel's ride!
  De plack man led de vay;
Dey reach de house—dey see de lights—
  Dey heard de fiddle blay.

Dey nefer vaited for a word,
  Boot galloped from de gloom,
Und *bang!*—a hoonderd carpine shots
  Dey fired into de room.
Oop vent de groans of vountet men,
  De fittlin died avay;
Boot some of dem vere tead before
  De music ceased to blay.

Den crack und smack coom scatterin shots
   Troo vindow und troo door,
Boot bang und clang de Germans gife
   Anoder volley more.
"Dere—let 'em shlide. Right file, to shoorsh!"
   Aloudt de orders ran.
"I kess I paid dem for dat shot!"
   Shpeak grim der Breitemann.

All rosen red de mornin fair
   Shone gaily o'er de hill,
All violet plue de shky crew teep
   In rifer, pond und rill.
All cloudy grey de limeshtone rocks
   Coom oop troo dimmerin wood;
All shnowy vite in mornin light
   De shoorsh pefore dem shtood.

"Now loudet vell de Organ oop,
   To drill mit solemn fear;
Und ring also dat Lumpenglock,
   To pring de beoples here.
Und if it prings guerillas down,
   Ve'll gife dem, py de Lord!
De low mass of de sabre, und
   De high mass of de cord!

"Du Eberlé aus Freiburg,
    Du bist ein Musikant.
Top-sawyer on de counter-point
    Und buster in discánt,
To dee de soul of music
    All innerly ish known,
Du canst mit might fullenden
    De art of orgel-ton.

"Derefore a Miserére
    Vilt dou, be-ghostet, spiel;
Und vake re-raiséd yearnin,
    Alsó a holy feel:—
Pe referent, men—rememper
    Dis ish a Gotteshaus—
Du, Conrad,—go along de aisles,
    Und schenk de whisky aus!"

Dey blay crate dings from Mozart,
    Beethoven und Méhul,
Mit chorals of Sebastian Bach,
    Sooplime und peaudiful.
Der Breitmann feel like holy saints,
    De tears roon down his fuss,
Und he sopped out: "Gott verdammich—dis
    Ist wahres Kunstgenuss!"

Der Eberlé blayed oop so high
  He make de rafters ring.
Der Eberlé blayed lower, und
  Ve heardt der Breitmann sing,
Like a dronin wind in piney woods,
  Like a nightly moanin sea,
Ash he dinked on Sonntags long agone
  Vhen a poy in Germany.

Und louder und mit louder tone
  High oop de orgel blowed,
Und plentifuller efer yet
  Around de whisky goed.
Dey singed ash if mit singin dey
  Might indo Himmel win :—
I dink in all dis land soosh shprees
  Ash yet hafe nefer peen.

Vhen in de Abendsonnenschein,
  Mit doost-cloudts troo de door,
All plack ash night in goldnen lighdt
  Dere shtood ein schwartzer Mohr.
Dat contrapand so wild und weh,
  Mit eye-palls glarin round,
Und cried: " For Gott's sake, hoory oop!
  De reps ish gomin down !"

Und vhile he yet vas shpeakin,
   A far-off soundt pegan,
Down rollin from de moundain,
   Of many a ridersmann.
Und vhile de waves of musik
   Vere rollin o'er deir heads,
Dey heard a foice a schkreemin:
   " Pile out of thar, you Feds!

"For we uns ar' a comin
   For to guv to you uns fits,
And knock you into brimstun,
   And blast you all to bits—"
Boot ere it done ids shpeakin
   Dere vas order in de band,
Ash Breitmann, mit an awefool stim
   Out-dondered his gommand.

Und ash fisch-hawk at a mackarel
   Doth make a splurgin flung,
Und ash eagles dab de fisch-hawks
   Ash if de gods were young;
So from all de doors und vindows,
   Like shpiders down deir webs,
De Dootch went at deir horses,
   Und de horses at de rebs.

Crate shplendors of de treadful
    Vere in dat pattle rush;
Crate vights mit swordt und carpine
    Py efery fence and bush;
Ash panters vight mit crislies
    In famished morder fits—
For de rebs vere mad ash boison,
    Und de Dootch ver droonk as blitz.

Yet vild ash vas dis pattle,
    So quickly vas it o'er:—
O vhy moost I forefer
    Pestain mine page mit gore
Py liddle und py liddle,
    Dey drawed demselfs afay;
Oft toornin round to vighten,
    Like booffaloes at bay.

De scatterin shots grew fewer,
    De scatterin gries more shlow;
Und furder troo de forest
    Ve heared dem vainter crow.
Ve gife von shout—" *Victoria!*"
    Und den der Breitmann said,
Ash he wiped his ploody sabre,
    "Now, poys, count oop your dead!"

O small had peen our shoutin
    For shoy, if ve had known,
Dat de Stossenheim im oaken Wald
    Lay dyin all alone;
Vhile his oldt white horse mit droopin het
    Look dumbly on him down,
Ash if he dinked, "Vy lyest dou here
    Vhile fightin's goin on?"

Und dreams coom o'er de soldier,
    Slow dyin on de cart,
Of a Schloss afar in Baden,
    Of his mutter, und nople birt—
Of poverty und sorrow
    Vhich drofe him like de wind—
Und he sighed: "Ach weh, for de lofed ones
    Who wait so far pehind!

"Wohl auf, my soul o'er de moundains!
    Wohl auf—well ofer de sea!
Dere's a frau dat sits in de Odenwald,
    Und shpins, und dinks of me.
Dere's a shild ash blays in de greenin grass,
    Und sings a liddle hymn,
Und learns to shpeak a fader's name
    Dat she nefer will shpeak to him.

"But mordal life ends shortly,
   Und Heafen's life is long—
Wo bist du, Breitmann?—glaub'es—
   Gott suffers no ding wrong.
Now I die like a Christian soldier;
   My head oopon my sword:—
In nomine Domine!"
   Vas Stossenheim his word.

O, dere vas bitter wailen
   Vhen Stossenheim vas found,
Efen from dose dere lyin
   Fast dyin on de grount.
Boot time vas short for vaiten,
   De shades vere gadderin dim;
Und I nefer shall forget it,
   De hour ve puried him.

De tramp of horse und soldiers
   Vas all de funeral knell,
De ring of sporn und carpine
   Vas all de sacrin bell.
Mit hoontin knife und sabre
   Dey digged de grave a span;
From German eyes blue gleamin
   De holy water ran.

Mit moss-grown shticks und bark-thong
 De plessed cross ve made,
Und put it vhere de soldier's head
 Toward Germany vas laid.
Dat grave is lost mid dead leafs,
 De cross is gone afay,
Boot Gott will find der reiter
 Oopon de Youngest Day.

Und dinkin of de fightin,
 Und dinkin of de dead,
Und dinkin of de Organ,
 To Nashville Breitmann led.
Boot long dat rough oldt Hanserl
 Vas ernsthaft, grim und kalt,
Shtill dinkin of de heart's friend,
 He'd left im gruenen Wald.

De verses of dis boem
 In Heidelberg I write.
De night is dark around me,
 De shtars apove are bright.
Studenten in den Gassen
 Make singen many a song,
Ach Faderland!—wie bist du weit!
 Ach Zeit!—wie bist du lang!

The First Edition of Breitmann.

Showing how and why it was that it never appeared.

> " *Uns ist in alten Maeren,*
> *Wunders viel geseit,*
> *Von Helden lobebaeren,*
> *Von grosser Arebeit,*
> *Von Festen und Hochzeiten,*
> *Von Weinen und Klagen,*
> *Von kuehnen Recken Streiten,*
> *Möht Ihr nun Wunderhören sagen.*"
>
> DER NIBELUNGEN LIED.

FIRSDT PARDT.

Do oos, in anciend shdory,
    Crate voonders ish peen told
  Of lapors fool of glories,
Of heroes bluff und bold,
Of high oldt times a-kitin,
  Of howlin und of tears,
Of kissin und of vightin:
  All dis we likes to hears.

Dere growed once dimes in Schwaben
    Since fifty years pegan,
An shild of decent elders,
    His name Hans Breitemann.
De gross adfentures dat he had,
    If you will only look,
Ish all bescribed so truly
    In dis fore-lying book.

Und allaweil dese lieder
    Vere goin troo his het,
De writer lay von Sonntay,
    A-shleepin in his bett;
Ven lo!—a yellow bigeon
    Coom to him in a dreám,
De same dat Mr. Barnum
    Vonce had in his Muséum.

Und dus out-shpoke de bigeon:
    "If you should brint de songs
Or oder dings of Breitmann
    Vhich to dem on belongs,
Dey will tread de road of Sturm und Drang
    Die wile es möhte leben,
Und pe mis-geborn in pattle
    To dis fate ish it ergeben."

Und dus rebly de dreamer:
"If on de ice it shlip,
Den led it dake ids shanses;
Rip Sam, und let 'er rip!
Dou say'st id vill be sturmy.—
Vot sturmy ish, ish crand.
Crate heroes ish de beoples
In Uncle Samuel's land.

Du bist ein rechter Gelbschnabel
O golden bigeon mine:
Und I'll fighdt id on dis summer
If id dakes me all de line.
Full liddle ish de discount
Oopon de Yankee peeps."
"Go to hell!" exglaim de bigeon:—
Foreby vas all mine shleeps.

SECONDT PARDT.

O ERE vent to Sout Carolina,
    A shentleman who dinked,
    Dat de pallads of der Breitmann
Should papered pe und inked.
Und dat he vouldt fixed de brintin
    Pefore de writer know:
Dis make to many a brinter
    Fool many a bitter woe.

All in de down of Charleston
    A druckerei he found,
Vhere dey cut de copy into takes,
    Und sorted it around.
Und all vas goot peginnen,
    For no man heeded mooch
Dat half de jours vas Mericans,
    Und half of dem vas Dutch.

Und vorser shtill, anoder half
    Had vorn de Federal plue,
Vhile de anti-half in Davis grey
    Had peen Confeterates true.
Great Himmel!—Vot a shindy
    Vos shtarted in de crowd
Vhen some von read Hans Breitmann
    His Barty all aloud!

Und von goot-nadured Yankee
  He schvear it vos a shame,
To dell soosh lies on Dutchmen,
  Und make of dem a game.
But dis make mad Fritz Luder,
  Und he schvear dis treat of Hans,
Vos shoost so goot a barty
  Ash any oder man's.

Und dat nodings vos so looscious,
  In all dis eartly shpear,
Ash a quart mug fool of sauer-kraut,
  Mit a plate of lager bier.
Dat de Yankee might pe tam mit himself
  For he, der Fritz, hafe peen
In many soosh a barty,
  Und all dose dings hafe seen.

All mad oopsproong de Yankee,
  Mid all his passion ripe,
Und vired at Fritz mit de shootin-shtick,
  Wheremit he vas settin type.
It hit him on de occiput,
  Und laid him on de floor;
For many a long day afder
  I ween his het vas sore.

Dis roused Piet Weiser der Pfaelzer,
    Who vas quick to act und dink;
He held in hand a roller
    Vhere-mit he vas rollin ink.
Und he dake his broof py shtrikin
    Der Merican top of his het,
Und make soosh a vine impression
    Dat he left de veller for deat.

Allaweil dese dings oonfolded,
    Dere vas rows of anoder kind,
Und drople in de wigwam
    Enough to trife dem plind;
Und a crate six-vooted Soutern man,
    Vot hafe vorked on a Refiew,
Shvear he hope to Gott he mighd pie de forms
    If de Breitmann's book warn't true.

For de Sout vas ploondered derriple,
    Und in dat darksome hour
He hafe lossed a yallow-pine maiden,
    Of all de land de vlower.
Bright gold doblones a hoondered
    He willingly vouldt pay,
Ash soon ash a thrip for a ginger-cake,
    Und deem it sheap dat day.

To him aut-worded a Yorker,
   Who shoomp den dimes de *boun-ti-ee*,
(De only dings *he* lossed in de war
   Was a sense of broperty :)
Says he, " Votefer *you* hafe dropped,
   Some oder shap hafe get,
Und de yallow-pine like him petter ash you;
   On dat it is safe to bet!"

Dead-pale pecame dat Soudern brave,
   He tidn't so moosh as yell;
Boot he drop right onto de Yorker,
   Und mit von lick bust his shell.
Den out he flashed his pig-sticker,
   Und mit looks of drementous gloom,
Rooshed vildly into de pattle
   Dat vas ragin round de room.

Boot, *in angulo*, in de corner,
   Anoder quarrel vas grow
Twix a Boston shap mit a Londoner,
   Und de row ish gekommen so:
De Yankee say dat de H-*u*-mor
   Of Breitmann vas less dan small;
Dough he maket de beoples laughen,
   Boot dat vas only all.

Den a Deutscher say by Donner!
　　Dat soosh a baradox
Vould leafe no hope for writers
　　In all Pandora's bænder box.
'Twas like de sayin dat Heine
　　Hafe no witz in him goot or bad;
Boot he only *kept sayin* witty dings,
　　To make beoples pelieve he had.

Den de oder veller be-headed
　　Dat dere vas not a shbark of foon
In de Breitmann lieds, vhen you lead dem
　　Into English correctly done:
Den a *Proof Sheet* veller res-pondered,
　　For he dink de dings vas hard;
" Dat ish shoost like de goot oldt lady
　　Ash vent to hear Artemas Ward.

" Und say it vas shames de beoples
　　Vas laugh demselfs most tead
At de boor young veller lecturin,
　　Vhen he tidn't know vot he said."
Hereauf de Yankee answered:
　　" Gaul dern it!—Shtop your fuss!"
Und all de crowd togeder
　　Go slap in a grand plug-muss.

De Yankee shlog de Proof Sheet
    Soosch an awfool smack on de face,
Dat he shvell rite oop like a poonkin
    Mit a sense of his tisgrace.
Boot a Deutscher boosted an ink-keg
    On dop of de oders hair,
It vly troo de air like a boomshell—denn—
    Mine Gotts!—Vot a sighdt vas dere!

Denn ofer all de shapel
    Vierce war vas ragin loose;
Fool many a vighten brinter
    Got well ge-cooked his goose;
Fool many an nose mit fisten
    I ween vas padly scrouged;
Fool many an eye pright-gleamin
    Vas ploody out-gegouged.

Dô wart ûfgehauwen
    Dere vas hewin off of pones.
Dô hôrte man dar inne
    Man heardt soosh treadful croans.
Jach waren dá die Geste
    De row vas rough und tough.
Genuoge sluogen wunden—
    Dere vas plooty wounds enough.

De shpirids of anciend brinters
　　From Himmel look down oopon,
Und allowed dat in a *chapel*
　　Dere vas nefer soosh carryins-on.
Dere vas Lorenz Coster mit Guttemberg,
　　Und Scheffer mit der Fust,
Und Sweynheim mit Pannartz trop deers
　　Oopon dis teufel's dust.

Dere vas Yankee jours extincted
　　Who lay oopon de vloor;
Dere vas Soutern rebs destructed
　　Who nefer vouldt Jeff no more.
Ash deir souls rise oop to Heafen,
　　Dey heard de oldt brinters calls;
Und Guttemberg gifed dem all a kick
　　Ash he histed dem ofer de walls.

Dat ish de vay dese Ballads
　　Foorst vere crooshed in plood und shdorm.
Fool many a day moost bass afay
　　Pefore dey dook dis form.
De copy flootered o'er de preasts
　　Of heroes lyin todt.
Dis vas de dire peginnin—
　　Das war des BREITMANN'S NOTH.

Dis song in Philadelphia
  Long dimes ago pegun;
In Paris vas gondinued, und
  In Dresden ist full-done.
If any toubt apout de *facts*
  In nople minds ish grew,
Let dem ashk Carl Benson Bristed—
  He knows id all ish druc.

Und now dese Breitmann shdories
  Ish geprindt in many a land,
Sogar in far Australia
  Dey're gestohlen und bekannt.
Geh hin mein Puch in alle VVelt,
  Steh auss was dir kompt zu.
Man beysse Dich, man reysse Dich,
  Nur dass man mir nichts thu.

Dranslation.

Go forth my book through all the world,
  Bear what thy fate may be!
They may bite thee, they may tear thee,
  So they do no harm to me!

I Gili Romaneskro.

A Gipsy Ballad.

WHEN der Herr Breitmann vas a yungling, he vas go, bummin aroundt, goot deal in de Worlt, vestigatin human natur, *roulant de vergne en vergne*, ash de Fraentsch boet says: "goin from town to town,"—seein beobles in gemixed sociedy, und learnin dose languages vitch ornamendt a drue moskopolite, or von whose het ish bemost mit experience. Mong oder tongues ash it would appeared, he shpoke fluendly Red Welsh, Black Dootch, Kauder-Waelsch Gaunersprache und Ghipsy, und dis latter languashe he pring so wide dat he write a pook of pallads in it—von of vitch pallads I have intuce him mit moush droples to telifer ofer to de worldt. De inclined reader, vill, mit crate heavy-hood blace pefore himself de fexation und lapor I hafe hat in der Breitmann his absents to get dese Shipsy verses broperly gorrected; as de only shentleman in town who vas culpable of so doin, ish peen gonfined in de town-brison; pout some drobles he hat for shdealin some hens, und pefore I couldt consoolt mit him, he vas rooned afay. Den I fond an oldt vomans Shipsy who vas do nodins boot peg, und so wider mit pout five or four oders more. Derfore der crordoms moast pe excused py de enlightened pooplic who are fomiliar mit dis peautiful languashe, vitch is now so shenerally fashionábel in literary und shpordin circles.

I Gili Romaneskro.

Schunava, ke baschko dela godla
    Schunava Paschomàskro.
Te del miro Dewel tumen
    Dschavena bachtallo.

Schunava apré to ruka
    Chirikló ke gillela:
Kamovéla but dives,
    Eh'me pale kamaveva.

A po je wa'wer divesseste
    Schunava pro gilaviben,
Mákana me avava,
    Pro marzos, pro kuriben.

So korava kuri bente
   So korava apre dróm;
Me kanáv miri romni,
   So kamela la lákero rom.

Dranslation.

I hear de gock a growin!
   I hear de musikant!
Gott gife dee a happy shourney
   Vhen you go to a distand landt.

I hears oopon de pranches
   A pird mit merry shdrain;
Goot many tays moost fanish
   Ere I coom to dis blace again.

Oopon some oder tay-times
   I'll hear dat song from dee;
Boot now I goes ash soldier,
   To war on de rollin sea.

Unt vot I shdeals in pattle,
   Und vot on de road I shdeal,
I'll pring all to my true lofe
   Who lofes her loafer so well.

Steinli von Slang.

FIRSDT PARDT.

Der Watchman look out from his tower,
    Ash de Abendgold glimmer grew dim,
    Und saw on de road troo de Gader
Ten shpearmen coom ridin to him:
Und he schvear: "May I lose my next bitter,
    Und denn mit der Teufel go hang,
If id isn't dat pully young Ritter,
    De hell-drivin Steinli von Slang."

"De vorldt nefer had any such man,
    He vights like a sturm in its wrath;
You may call me a recular Dutchmann,
    If he arn't like Goliath of Gath.
He ish pig ash de shiant O'Brady,
    More ash sefen feet high on a string,
Boot he can't vin de hearts of my lady,
    De lofely Plectruda von Sling."

De lady makes welcome her gast in,
    Ash he shtep to de dop of de shtairs;
She look like an angel got lost in
    A forest of autumn-brown hair.
Und a bower-maiden said as she tarried:
    "I wish I may bust mit a bang!
If id isn't a shame she ain't married
    To der her-re-liche Steinli von Slang!"

He pows to de cround fore de lady,
    Vhile his vace ish ash pale ash de tead;
Und she vhispers oonto him a rédè,
    Ash mit arrow point accents she said:
"You hafe long dimes peen dryin to win me,
    You hafe vight, und mine braises you sing;
Boot I'm 'fraid dat de notion ain't in me."—
    De lady Plectruda von Sling.

"Boot brafe-hood teserfes a reward, Sir:
    Dough you've hardly a chost of a shanse.
Sankt Werolf!—medinks id ish hardt, Sir,
    I should allaweil lead you dis dance."
Like a bees ven it booz troo de clofer,
    Dese murmurin accents she flang,
Vhile singin, a stingin her lofer—
    Der woe-moody Ritter von Slang.

" Boot if von ding you do, I'll knock under,
　　Our droples moost enden damit;
　Und if you pull troo it,—by donder!
　　I'll own myself euchred und bit.
　I schvear py de holy Sanct Chlody!
　　Py mine honor—und avery ding!
　You may hafe me—soul, puttons und pody,
　　Mit de whole of Plectruda von Sling.

" Und dis ish de test of your power:—
　　Vhile ve shtand ourselfs round in a row,
　You moost roll from de dop of dis tower
　　Down shtairs to de valley pelow.
　Id ish rough und ash shteep ash my virtue:
　　(Mit schwanen shweet accents she sang:)
" Tont dry if you dinks it vill hurt you,
　　Mine goot liddle Ritter von Slang."

An moormoor arosed mong de beoples;
　　In fain tid she doorn in her shcorn.
Der votchman on dop of de shdeeples
　　Plowed a sorryfool doon on his horn.
Ash dey look down de dousand-foot treppé,
　　Dey schveared dey vouldt pass on de ding,
Und not roll down de firstest tam steppé
　　For a hoondred like Fraeulein von Sling.

SECONDT PARDT.

TWAS Audumn. De dry leafs vere bustlin
  Und visperin deir elfin-wild talk,
  Ven shlow, mit his veet in dem rustlin,
Herr Steinli coomed out for a walk.
Wild dooks vly afar in de gloamin,
  He hear a vaint gry vrom de gang;
Und vished he vere off mit dem roamin—
  De heart-wounded Ritter von Slang.

Und ash he vent musin und shbeakin,
  He see, shoost aheat in his vay,
In sinkular manner a streakin,
  An strange liddle pein, in cray,
Who toorned on him quick mit a holler,
  Und cuttin a dwo-bigeon ving,
Gried: "Say—can you change me a thaler,
  O, guest of de Lady von Sling?"

De knight vas a goot nadured veller,
  (De peggars all knowed him at sight,)
So he forked out each groschen und heller
  Dill he fix de finances aright.
Boot shoost ash de liddle man vent, he
  (Der Ritter) astonished, cried "Dang!"
For id vasn't von thaler boot *twenty*
  He'd bassed on der Ritter von Slang.

Oh reater!—soopose soosh a vlight in
   De vingers of me, or of you,
How we'd toorned on our heels und gon kitin
   Dill no von vas left to pursue!
Goot Lort!—how *we'd* froze to de ready!
   Boot mit him 'dvas a different ding;
For *he* vent on de high, moral steady,
   Dis lofer of Fraeulein von Sling.

Und dough no von vill gife any gredit
   To dis part of mine dale, shdill ids drue,
He drafelled, ash if he vould *dead* it,
   Dis liddle oldt man to pursue.
Und loudly he after him hollers,
   Till de vales mit de cliffers loud rang,
"You hafe gifed me nine-ten too moosh dollars—
   Hold hard!" cried de Ritter von Slang.

De oldt man ope his eyes like a casement,
   Und laidt a cold hand on his prow,
Denn mutter in ootmosdt amazement:
   "Vot manner of mordal art dou?
I hafe lifed in dis world a yar tausend,
   Und nefer yed met soosh a ding;
Yet you find it hart vork to pe spouse und
   Peloved py de Lady von Sling!

"Und she vant you to roll from de tower
   Down shteps to yon rifulet shpot."
(Here de knight whom amazement o'erbower
   Gried " Himmelspotzpumpenherr Gott!")
Boot de oldt veller saidt: "I'll arrange it.
   Let your droples und sorrows co hang!
Und no dings vill coom to derange it,
   Pet high on it, Ritter von Slang."

"So get oop dis small oonderstandin;
   Dat to-morrow py ten—do you hear?—
You'll pe mit your *trunk* on de landin;
   I'll pe dere on hand, nefer fear.
Und I dink ve shall make your young voman
   A new kind of meloty sing;—
Dat vain, vicked, cruel, unhuman,
   Gott tamnaple Fraeulein von Sling!"

De fiolet shdars vere apofe him,
   Vhite moths und vhite dofes shimmered round,
All nature seemed seekin to lofe him,
   Mit perfume und vision und sound.
De liddle oldt feller hat fanished
   In a harp-like melotious twang;
Und mit him all sorrow vas panished
   Afay from der Steinle von Slang.

THIRDT PARDT.

Id vas morn, und de vorldt hat assempled
  Mit panners und lances und dust,
Boot de heart of de Paroness trempled,
  Und ofden her folly she cussed.
For she found dat der Ritter vould *do it*,
  Und "die or get into de Ring;"
Und denn she'd pe cerdain to rue it,
  Aldough she vas Lady von Sling.

For no man in Deutschland stood higher
  Dan he mit de Minnesing crew;
He vas friendet to Heini von Steier,
  Und Wolfram von Eschenbach too.
Und she dinked ash she look from de vinders,
  How herzlich his braises dey sang;
"Now dey'll knock my goot name indo flinders
  For killin der Ritter von Slang."

Boot oh! der goot knight had a schauer,
  Und felt most ongommonly queer,
Ven he find on de dop of de dower
  De gray man pesite him appear.
Den he find he no more could go valkin,
  Und shtood shoost an potrified ding,
Vhile de gray man vent round apout talkin
  Und chaflin Plectruda von Sling!

Den at vonce he see indo de problum,
   Und vas stoggered like rats at ids *vim;*
His soul had gone indo de goblum,
   Und de goblum's hat gone into him.
Und de eyes of de volk vas enchanted,
   Dere vas " glamour " oopon de whole gang,
For dey dinked dat dis goblum vitch ranted
   So loose, vas der Ritter von Slang.

Und Lordt! *how* id dalked! Oonder heafens
   Der vas nefer soosh derriple witz,
Knockin all dings to sechses und sefens,
   Und gifin Plectruda Dutch fits.
Mein Gott! how he poonished und chaffed her,
   Like a hell-stingin, devil-born ding,
Vhile de volk lay a-rollin mit laughter
   At Fraeulein Plectruda von Sling.

De lady grew angry und paler,
   De lady grew rat-full und red,
She felt some Satanical jailer
   Hafe brisoned de tongue in her head.
She moost laugh ven she vant to pe cryin,
   Und vas crushed mit de teufelisch clang,
Till she knelt herself, pootty near dyin,
   To dis derriple image of Slang.

Den der goblum shoomp oop to der cicling,
   Und trow sommerseds round on de vloor,
Right ofer Plectruda, a-kneelin,
   Dill she look more a vool dan pefore.
Denn he roll down de shteps light und breezy,
   His laughs made it all apout ring,
Ash he shveared dere vas noding more easy
   Dan to win a Plectruda von Sling.

Und ven he cot down to de pottom,
   He laugh so to freezen your plood;
Und schwear dat de boomps ash he cot em
   Hafe make him veel petter ash good.
Boot—oh—how dey shook at his power,
   Ven he toorned himself roundt mit a bang,
Und roll oop to de dop of de tower
   Vhere he change mit de oder von Slang!

Den all in an insdand vas altered;
   Der Steinli vas coom to himself;
Und de sprite, vitch in double sense paltered,
   From dat moment acain vas an elf.
Dey shdill dinked dat von Slang vas de person
   Who had bobbed oop und down on de ving,
Und knew not who 'tvas lay de curse on
   De peaudiful Lady von Sling.

Nun—endlich—Plectruda—repented,
  Und gazed on der Ritter mit shoy;
In dime to pe married consented,
  Und vas plessed mit a peautiful poy.
A dwenty gold biece on his bosom
  Ven geporn vas tiscofered to hang,
Mit de inscript—" Dis dime don't refuse em."—
  So endet de tale of von Slang.

To a Friend Studying German.

Si liceret te amare,
Ad Suevorum magnum mare
Spousam te perducerem.
[*Tristicia Amorosa. Frau Aventiure, von J. V. Scheffel.*]

Will'st dou learn de Deutsche Sprache?
  Den set it on your card
  Dat all de nouns have shenders,
Und de shenders all are hard.
Dere ish also dings called pronoms,
  Vitch ids shoost ash vell to know;
Boot ach!—de verbs or time-words,
  Dey'll work you bitter woe.

Vill'st dou learn de Deutsche Sprache?
   Denn you allatag moost go
To sinfonies, sonatas,
   Or an oratorio.
Ven you dinks you knows 'pout musik,
   More ash any oder man,
Pe sure de soul of Deutschland
   Indo your soul ish ran.

Vill'st dou learn de Deutsche Sprache?
   Dou moost eat apout a peck
A week of stinging sauer-kraut,
   Und sefen pfoundts of shpeck;
Mit Gott knows vot in vinegar,
   Und Deuce knows vot in rum:
Dis ish de only cerdain vay
   To make de accents coom.

Vill'st dou learn de Deutsche Sprache?
   Brepare dy soul to shtand
Soosh sendences ash n'er vere heardt
   In any oder landt.
Till dou canst bear parentheses
   Pe twisted ohne Zahl;
Dann wirst du erst Deutschfertig seyn
   For a languashe ideál.

Vill'st dou learn de Deutsche Sprache?
   Du moost, mitout an fear,
Trink efery tay a gallon dry
   Of foamin Sherman bier.
Und de more you trinks, pe cerdain,
   More Deutsch you'll surely pe,
For Gambrinus ish de Emberor
   Of de whole of Germany.

Vill'st dou learn de Deutsche Sprache?
   Pe sholly, brav und treu,
For dat veller ish kein Deutscher
   Who ish not a sholly poy;
Find out vot means Gemüthlichkeit,
   Und try it mitout fail,
In Sang und Klang dein Lebenlang,
   A heart, ganz kreuzfidél.

Vill'st dou learn de Deutsche Sprache?
   If a shendleman dou art,
Denn shdrike right into Deutschland,
   Und get a shveetesheart
From Schwabenland or Sachsen,
   Vhere now dis writer pees,
Und de bretty girls all wachsen
   Shoost like aepples on de drees.

Boot if dou bee'st a lady,
   Denn on de oder hand,
Take a blonde moustachioed lofer,
   In de vine-green Sherman land.
Und if you shouldt kit married,
   Vood mit vood soon makes a vire:
O denn you'll find de Dutch vill coom
   Ash fast as you desire.

Love Song.

O VERE mine lofe a sugar-powl,
   De fery shmallest loomp
   Vouldt shveet de seas from bole to bole,
Und make de shildren shoomp.
Und if she vere a clofer-fieldt,
   I'd bet mine only pence,
It vould'nt pe no dime at all
   Pefore I'd shoomp de fence.

Her heafenly foice it drill me so,
    It really seems to hoort;
She ish de holiest anamile
    Dat roons oopon de dirt.
De re'nbow rises ven she sings,
    De sonn shine ven she dalk,
De angels crow und flop deir vings
    Ven she goes out to valk.

So livin vhite—so carnadine—
    Mine lofe's gomblexion glow;
It's shoost like abendcarmosine
    Rich gleamin on de shnow.
Her soul makes plooshes in her sheek,
    As sommer reds de wein,
Or sonlight sends a fire-life troo
    An blank karfunkelstein.

De ueberschwengliche idées
    Dis lofe put in my mind,
Vould make a foostrate philosoph
    Of any human kind.
'Tis shuderend sweet on eart' to meet
    An himmlisch-hoellisch qual,
Und treat mit whiles to kümmel schnapps
    De Shœnheitsideál.

GLOSSARY.

Abendgold, (German)—Evening gold.
Abendsonnenschein, (German)—Evening sunshine.
Ach Fuderland, &c., (German)—
"Oh Fatherland how far art thou!
Oh Time—how art thou long!"
Ach weh—An exclamation of pain.
Allatag, (German)—Every day.
Allaweil, (German)—Always; also whilst.
Alles wird ewig zu eins, (German)—And all for ever becomes one.
Alter Schwed', (old Swede)—A familiar phrase, like old fellow.
Anamile, (American)—Animal.
Annerthalb Yar, Anderthalb Gahr, (German)—Year and a half.
Anti Word; Antwort—Answer.
Antworded, (German)—Answered.
Arbeiterhalle—Workingman's hall.
Arminius, (Herman.)—The Duke of the Cheruskans, and destroyer of the Roman legions under Varus, in Teutoburg Forest.
Aroom, Herum—Around.
Aufgespannt, (German)—Stretched, bent.
Augenblick, (German)—Twinkling of an eye.
Aus, (German)—Out.

Bach, (German)—Brook.
Baender-box—Band-box.
Barrick, (Pennsylvania German for *Berg*,)—Mountain.
Barrel-hell pars—Parallel bars; a part of the gymnastic apparatus.
Be-ghostet, (German, *Begeistert*)—Inspired.
Begifted—Beschenkt.
Begreifen, (German)—Understand.
Beheaded, (German, *Behauptet*)—Asserted.
Bei Leib und Leben, (German)—By my body and soul.
Bekannt Beknown—Known.
Be-mark, (German *Bemerken*)—Observe.
Bemarks, (German, *Bemerkungen*)—Remarks.
Bemerkbar, (German) Observable. (Should be noticed.)
Bemoost, (German)—Mossgrown; in student's language, *ein bemooste Haupt*, an old student.
Bender, (American)—A spree; a frolic. To "go on a *bender*"—to go on a spree.
Be-raised, Raised, with the augment, literal for German *erhoben*.
Berauscht, (German)—Intoxicated.
Besoffen, (German)—Drunk.
Bestimmung des Menschen—Vocation of Man. One of Fichte's works.
Bewises, (German *Beweist*, from *Beweisen*)—Proves.
Bibliothek—Library.
Bix, Büchse, (box)—Rifle. Bess in Brown Bess is the equivalent of the German *Büchse*, (Brown being merely an alliterative epithet;) French, *buse tube;* Flemish, *buis*. (Still found in blunderbuss, arquebuss.) See Blackley's "Word Gossip."
Blaetter, (German)—Leaves.
Blei—Lead.
Blitz, (German)—Lightning.
Blitzen, German)—Lightning.
Blokes, (English)—Men.
Bock—A strong kind of German beer.
Boemisch—Bohemian.
Bole Jack road—Near Murfreesboro', Tennessee.

Bool—Bull.
Bornirtheit—Limitedness of capacity.
Bountiee, (American)—Bounty-money paid during the war as a premium to soldiers. To jump the bounty, was to secure the premium and then run away.
  "This is the song of Billy Jones,
    Who jumped the boun-ti-ec."
              American Ballad of 1864.
Bowery—A street in New York, inhabited principally by Germans.
Brav, (German)—Good.
Breit, (German)—Broad.
Bring it down to dots—Reduce it to figures.
Brisner—Prisoner.
Broosh-pinder—Brushbinder, (German, *Buerstenbinder*)—Brushmaker. The brushmakers are supposed, probably on account of their throat-parching business, to be always thirsty.
Brummed, (German, *Crummer*)—To make a growling, deep bass sound.
Bummer, (American)—A low fellow; applied, during the late civil war in the United States, to hangers-on of the army; probably a corruption of the German *bummler*, (loafer.)
Bumming—From Bummer.
Bushwhackers—Guerillas.
Bust his shell, (American)—Broke his head.
Butterbrod, (German)—Buttered bread.
By—Nearly; *Beinahe*—Almost, nearly.
Came—Game.
Canyon, (Spanish, *Cañon*)—A narrow passage between high precipitous banks, formed by mountains or tablelands, often with a river running beneath. These occur in the great Western prairies, in New Mexico, and California.
Carmosine, (German)—Crimson. French—Cramoisie.
Carnadine—Incarnadine. Deep pink or blood red.
Change their lodge—Shift from one "society" to another.

Chroc—An Alemannic hero, who ravaged Gaul. Spoken of by Gregory, of Tours, as Chrocus.
Chunk—A short thick piece of wood, or of anything else; a chump. The word is provincial in England and colloquial in the United States.
Cinder, Suende—German for sins.
Comedy—Committee.
Conradin—The last of the imperial house of the Hohenstaufen—beheaded at Naples, in 1268.
Coot—(To cut) a dash, (to come out a "swell,") to dress extravagantly.
Coster—The inventor of the art of printing, according to the Dutch.
Crate—Great.
Crislies—Grisly, (bear.)
Da ist er! Schau!—There he is! look!
Damit, (German)—By that.
Das war des Breitmann's Noth, (German)—That was Breitmann's need or fatal extremity. Imitated from the last line of Der Nibelungen Lied.
Deck—The cards used in a game.
Demperanceler, Temperenzler—Temperance man.
De Schœnheitsidéal, (German)—The ideal of beauty.
Dessauerinn—A woman from Dessau.
Deutschfertig, (German) — German-ready. A burlesque word. "Then you will be German-ready for an ideal perfect language."
Deutschland—Germany.
Die wile es möhte leben, (Old German, or Middle High German of the 11th century)—During all its life:—
"Daz wolde er immer dienen
Die wile er möhte leben."
Kutrun, xv avent, 756 verse.
Dink—He, they think; *my dinks*—my thoughts.
Dinked—He, they thought.
Dishtriputet—Instead of *attributed*.
Dissembulatin'—Dissembling.
Dissolfed—Instead of *resolved*.
D'lusion—Instead of *allusion*.

Donnered, (German)—Thundered.
Donnerwetter, (German)—Thunder and lightning.
Dooks—Ducks.
Doon—Tune.
Doonderblix—Thunder and lightning.
Drawed he in—(Literal rendering of the German *Zog er ein*) —*Einziehen*, to take up one's abode with.
Dreimal, (German)—Three times.
Drocks—Drakes, dragons; (German)—Drachen.
Druckerei, (German)—Printing office.
Du bist ein Musikant—Thou art a musician.
Dummehrlichkeit, (German)—Honest simplicity.
Eberschwein, (German)—Wild boar.
Einander to sprechen mit, (German)—To speak together.
Eldern, (German, *Eltern*)—Parents.
Elders, (German, *Eltern*)—Parents.
Elfenbein, (German)—Ivory.
Emerich—King Emerich, hero of a German legend.
Emsig gruebler, (German)—Assidious inquirer; plodding old fogy.
Entlang, (German)—Along.
Erfounden, (German, *Erfunden*)—Invented.
Ergeben, (German)—Given over.
Ernsthaft, (German)—Earnest.
Error-dom, *Irrthum*—Error.
Erstarrt, (German)—Aghast.
Erstaunished, *erstaunt*—Astonished!
Erwaitin', (German, *Erwartend*)—Awaiting, expecting.
Euchred—From Euchre, a Western game of cards.
Fackel Tanz, (German)—Torch dance.
Fancy crabs—Fast horses.
Fanes, *Wetterfahnen*—Weathercocks, (double entente.)
Fass, (German)—Barrel.
Fat—Printer's term.
Feldwebel, (German)—A sergeant.
Fichte—German philosopher.
Finster, (German)—Dark, dismal.
Foll—To fall.
Fool—Full.

Foon—Fun.
Foors—First.
Fore-by—Literal translation of the German *Vorbei*.
Fore-lying—Literal translation of *Vorliegend*.
Foreschlag, (German, *Vorschlag*)—Proposal.
Foresetzen—To set, put (lay) before an audience.
Frau, (German)—Woman.
Freie, (German)—Free.
Freischarlinger, (German, *Freischaerler*)—A member of a free corps; especially applied to those who belonged to the Free Corps formed in Southern Germany during the revolution in 1848.
Freischuetz, (German)—Free shot; one who shoots with charmed bullets; the name of Karl Maria Von Weber's celebrated opera.
Friederich Rothbart—Frederic Barbarossa, the great emperor of Germany, and one of the German Legendary heroes. He is supposed to sleep in the Kyffnauser in Thuringia, and to awaken one day, when he will bring great glory over Germany.
Frolic—Fröhlich, merry.
Froze to de ready—Held fast to the money.
Fullenden, (German, *Vollenden*)—To finish, perfect.
Fuss, (German)—Foot.
Fust—The partner of Gutemberg, the inventor of the art of printing.
Gambrinus—A mythical king of Brabant, supposed to have been the inventor of beer.
Gandertate—Candidate.
Ganz, (German)—Entirely.
Ganz und gar, (German)—Altogether; all over.
Gast, (German)—Guest.
Gauer—Vallies.
Gaul dern—A Yankee oath.
Gauner-sprache, (German)—Thieves' language.
Ge-birt', (German, *Geburt*)—Birth.
Ge-bildet—Built, with the German augment.
Geborn—Born, with the augment.
Ge-brudert, (formed like ge-schwister.)—Brothers.

Geh hin mein Puch, (German of 16th century.)
Gehst nit mit rechten Dingen zu—Dost not do it by any natural means; there is witchcraft in it.
Gekommene—Arrived, (newly arrived.)
Gekommen so, (German)—Come thus.
Gelbschnabel, (German)—Yellow bill, (*i. e.* soft.) Meaning a "greenhorn."
Gelt, (German, *Geld*)—Money.
Gemüthlichkeit, (German)—Good nature; a cheerful tone of mind.
Gensy broost, (German, *Gänsebrust*)—Goose-breast.
Ge-roasted—Roasted, with German augment.
Gesembled—Assembled, with the augment of the German preterite.
Geshmasht—Smashed, with German augment.
Gespicked, (German)—Larded.
Gestohlen und bekannt, (German)—Stolen, and known.
Gesundheit, (German)—Health.
Gesangverein, (German)—Singing-society.
Geskostet—Cost, with the German augment.
Gilt—In the ordinary sense, and also in the same verse, "*gilt*," implying the meaning of the German verb "*gelten*," to be worth something and *guilt*.
Glaub'es, (German)—Believe it.
Glee-wine, *Gluhwein*—Hot spiced wine.
Glueck, (German)—Luck.
Glucky, (German, *Gluecklich*)—Lucky.
Goblum—For goblin.
Gool—Cool.
Go screech, *Geschrei*—Bawling, clamour.
Gott-full, *gottvoll*—Glorious, divine.
Gottallmachty, (German, *Gottallmächtig*)—God Almighty.
Gotteshaus, (German)—House of God.
Gott weiss, (German)—Heaven knows!
Gottsdonnerkreuzschockschwerenoth, (German)—Another variety of big swearing.
Gott's-doonder, (German, *Gott's Donner*)—God's thunder. See also *Gott's tausend*, a thundering sort of oath, but never preceded by lightning, for it is only used as a

kind of expletive to express great surprise, or to give great emphasis to words which, without it, would seem to be capable of none.

Gottstausend, (German)—An abbreviation of *Gott's tausend Donnerwetter*, (God's thousand thunders,) and therefore the comparative of *Gott's doonder;* with most of those who use it, a meaningless phrase.

Go von—Go one; bet on him.

Grillers—Guerillas.

Grod, gerard—Straight.

Gross, (German)—Great.

Guestfriendllick, gastfreundlich—Hospitable.

Gummi lasticum—India Rubber.

Gutemberg—The inventor of the art of printing.

Guve—Southern slang for give. *Guv*, for give, is also English slang as well as American.

Gyrotwistive—Snaky.

Hand-shoe, (German, *Handschuh*)—Glove.

Hanserl, (German)—Jacky.

Hans Wurst—Merry Andrew; Zani; Jack Pudding—the latter word being a literal translation of the German Hans Wurst; the pudding in either case referring to the sausages, or the pretended sausages, which the Merry Andrew always appeared to be swallowing by the yard or fathom. See *Blackley's Word Gossip.*

Hagel! Blitz! Kreuz Sakrament! (German)—Another variety of swearing.

Haul te pot—Take the stakes.

Hause—House.

Heavy—Hood.

Hegel—Name of the German philosopher.

Heine, Heinrich—German poet.

Heini von Steier—Heinrich von Opterdingen.

Heldenbuch—Is the title of a collection of epic poems, belonging to the cycle of the German Saga.

Heller Glorie schein—Bright gloriole.

Heller, (German)—*Farthing.*

Hereauf, hierauf—Thereupon.

Herout, (German, *Heraus*)—Out.

Herrlich, (German)—Noble ; lordly.
Herr Je, (German)—An abbreviation of *Herr Jesus* (O Lord !) ; generally used only by those who are fond of meaningless exclamations.
Hexerei—Witchery, sorcery.
Hertszen—Herzen ; hearts.
Hertzhog, Herzog, (German)—Duke.
Herzlich, (German)—Heartily ; cordially.
Himmel, (German)—Heaven.
Himmels-Potz-Pumpen-Herrgott—A mild sort of a German imprecation, untranslatable.
Himmlisch-hoellisch qual, (German)—Heavenly-hellish pain.
Hobbiness—Happiness.
Hoellisch, (German)—Hellish.
Honey foolin', Honeyfuggle—Is believed to be **English** slang. In America it means blarneying, deceiving.
Hoockle *perry, Persimmoned*—"A huckleberry over my persimmon." Surpassed ; outdone.
Hoof-irons, (*Huf-eisen* in German)—Horse-shoe.
Hop-sossa, (German) int.—Hop ; heyday.
Hundsfott, (German *Vulg.*)—Mean scoundrel ; hound.
Hunk, (American)—Stout, solid, profitable.
I Gili romaneskro. This song is written in the German-Gipsy dialect. *Eh'* in the third line of the second verse is the German word ehe, (ere or before.) *Kuribente*, (in war,) is in the Slavonic and Gipsy *local* case, or as Pott calls it—(*Die Zigennen in Europa und Asia*)—The second dative. Pasputi, following Puchmayer, calls it the first dative, as *e rakleste* "in the child."
Im gruenen Wald, (German)—In the green wood.
Im Oaken Wald, (German)—In the oak wood.
In nomine Domine, (Latin)—In the name of the Lord ;
  "In nomine Domine!
   Was Hero Hagen's word."
In Sang und Klang dein Lebenlang. In song and music all thy life.
Jeff, (printer's phrase)—A game played by throwing up types and counting the nicks.

Joss-stick—A name given to small reeds, covered with the dust of odoriferous woods, which the Chinese burn before their idols.
Jours—Journeymen.
Jungfernkranz, (German)—Bridal garland.
Kœnig Etzel—King Attila.
Kaiser Karl—Charlemagne.
Kalt, (German)—Cold.
Kanaster, (German)—Canaster tobacco.
Karfunkelstein, (German)—Carbuncle.
Kartoffell, (German)—Potato.
Kauder-Waelsch, (German)—Gibberish.
Kellner, (German)—Waiter.
Kinder, (German)—Children.
Kitin, a kitin—Flying or running rapidly.
Knasterbart, (German)—Literally, tobacco-beard; a tough, old bearded, old-fashioned fellow.
Kneiperei, (German)—Revel.
Knock dem out de shpots—Knock the spots out of them; astonish.
Komm maidelein! Rothe Waengelein, (German)—Come, maiden, red cheeks.
Kop, (German *Kopf*)—Head.
Kreutzer,—Fr. Creutzer, distinguished professor in the University of Heidelberg, author of a great work on "Symbolik."
Kreuzfidel, (German)—True-hearted; gallant in the highest degree.
Krumm, (German)—Crooked. *Breit und Krumm*—Broad and crooked. Here, a pun on bride and groom.
Kümmel, (German) Cumin brandy.
Kummel Kimmel, (German)—Schnapps; dram.
Lager, Lagerbeer, (German *Lagerbier*, i. e. *Stockbeer*.)
Lager Wirthschaft, (German)—Beerhouse.
Lam—To drub; to beat soundly.
Lateinisch—Latin.
Laughen, lachen—Laughing.
Lavergne—A place between Nashville and Murfreesboro', in the State of Tennessee.

Lebenlang, (German)—Lifelong.
Leider, *Leids*, (German)—Songs.
Libby—The notorious Confederate prison at Richmond, Va.
Liddle Pills—Legislative enactments.
Liederkranz, (German)—Glee-union.
Liederlich, (German)—Loose, reckless, dissolute.
Lighthood, (German *Lichtheif*)—Licht.
Like spiders down their webs—Breitmann's soldiers are supposed to have been expert turners or gymnasts.
Loafer—A term which, considered as the German pronunciation of *lover*, is a close translation of *rom*, as this latter means both a Gipsy and a husband.
Loosty, (German *Lustig*)—Jolly: merry.
Los, los gehen, (German)—To go at a thing, at somebody.
Loudet, (*Lauten* in German)—To make sound.
Lump, (German)—Ragamuffin.
Lumpenglocke, (German)—An abusive term applied to bells, especially to those which give the signal that the beer houses must close.
Maedchen, (German)—Girl; maiden.
Mákana, (Gipsy, *Ma akana*)—But now.
"*Make de red cock crow*"—"To set the red cock on the roof," signifies in German, to set a man's house on fire.
Marmorbild—Marble statue.
Markgraefler—A pleasant light wine grown in the Duchy of Baden.
Maskenzug, (German)—Procession of masked persons.
Massenversammlung, (German)—Mass meeting.
Mein Freund—My Friend.
Meine Seel', (German)—By my soul.
Mineted—Minded.
Minnesinger—Poet of love; a name given to German lyric poets, who flourished from the twelfth to the fourteenth centuries.
Mit hoontin knife, &c.—
"With her white hands so lovely
She dug the Count his grave,
From her dark eyes sad weeping,
The holy water she gave."
(Old German ballad.)

Mitout—Without
Mitternocht, Mitternacht—Midnight.
Mitternight, Mitternacht—Midnight.
Mitz hauf, (German)—Dung-hill.
Moleschott—Author of a celebrated work on Physiology.
Morgan—John Morgan, a notorious Confederate guerilla during the late war in America.
Morgen-het-ache—Morning headache.
Moskopolite—(American)—Cosmopolite.
Murmulte—Murmured.
Mutter, (German)—Mother.
Nieblungen Lied—The lay of the Nieblungen; the great German national epos.
Nix, (German, *Nichts*)—Nothing.
Nix cum raus—Had not come out.
Norate—To speak in an oration.
No sardine—Not a narrow-minded, small-hearted fellow.
Noth, (German)—Need, dire extremity. Das war des Breitmann's noth. That was Breitmann's sore trial. Imitated from the last line of the *Niebelungen Lied.*
Nun—Now.
Nun-endich, (German)—Well, at last.
O'Brady—An Irish giant commemorated in a once popular song.
Oder—Other.
Odenwald—A thickly-wooded district in South Germany.
Ohne Zhal, (German)—Without number.
On-belongs—Literal translation of *Zugehört.*
On-did, to *on-do*—Literal translation of the German anthem; *to dun,* to put on.
On de snap—All at once.
Onfang, (German, *Anfang*)—Beginning.
Oonshpeakbarly, (German, *unanssprechbarlich*)—Inexpressibly.
Oonendly—Undenlich.
Oop-gecleared, (German, *Aufgeklaert*)—Enlightened.
Oopright-hood, (German, *Aufrichtigkeit*)—Uprightness.
Ooprighty, (German, *Aufrichtig*)—Upright.
Oopshtardet, (German, *Aufgeschärft*)—Upstarted.

Oop-sproong—For *aufsprung*.
Orgel-ton, (German)—Organ sound.
Orkester—Orchestra.
Out-sprach—Outspoke.
Out-signed, (German, *ausgezeichnete*)—Distinguished, signal.
Over again—*Uebringen*—The remainder ; a rest.
Pabst, Der Pabst lebt, &c.—" The Pope he leads a happy life," &c., beginning of a popular German song.
Peeps—People. "Hard on the American peeps"—a phrase for anything exacting or severely pressing.
Pelznickel, Nick, Nickel!—St. Nicolas is supposed, on the night preceding his name-day, the sixth of December, to pass over the house-tops on his long-eared steed, having baskets suspended on either side filled with sweets and playthings, and to drop down through the chimneys presents for those children who have been good during the year, but birch-rods for those who have been naughty, would not go to bed early, or objected to being washed, &c. In the expectation of his coming, the children put, on the eve of St. Nicolas day, either a shoe, or a stocking, or a little basket into the chimney-piece of their parents' bed-room. We may remark, by the way, that St. Nicolas is the Christian successor of the heathen Nikudr, of ancient German mythology. In America he has become confused with Christkinder and Christkinkel.
Pesser, besser, (German)—Better.
Pestain—Stain, with the augment.
Pfaelzer—A man from the Rhenish Palatinate.
Pfeil, (German)—Arrow.
Philosopede—Velocipede.
Pie the forms—Break up and scatter the forms of type.
Pig-sticker, (American)—Bowie-knife, or indeed, any other kind of knife.
Pile out, (American)—Hurry out.
Plue goats—Blue coats ; soldiers.
Plug muss, (American Fireman)—A fight around a fire-plug.

Pokal, (Poculum)—Goblet.
Poker—A favorite game of cards among Western gamblers.
Poonkin—Pumpkin.
Potzausend! Was ist das?—Zounds! What is that?
Potzblitz, (German)— int., The deuce.
Poulterie—Poultry.
Poussiren—To court.
Pretzel, (German)—A kind of fancy bread, twist or the like.
Prezackly—Pre(cisely,) exactly.
Protocollirt, protocolliren—To register, record.
Pumpernickel—A heavy, hard sort of rye-bread.
Pye—To buy.
Raushlin', rauschend—Rustling.
Reb—An abbreviation of rebel.
Redakteur—Editor.
Rede, (German)—Speech.
Rede, (German)—Speech.
Red-Waelsch, Roth-Wae sch, (German)—Thieves' language.
Reiter, (German)—Rider.
Rheinweinbechers Klang—The Rhine wine goblet's sound.
Richter, (Jean Paul, French)—Distinguished German author.
Ridersmann, (*Reitersmann* in German)—Rider.
Ring—A political clique or cabal.
Ritter, (German)—Knight.
Roland—One of the paladins of Charlemagne.
Rollin' locks—Rolling logs; mutually aiding.
Rosen, (German)—Roses.
Rouse, (German *Heraus*)—Out; come out.
Sachsen—Saxonia, Saxony.
Sacrin—Consecrating.
Sagen Cyclus—Cycle of legends.
Sass, Sassy, Sassin'—Sauce, saucy, &c.
Sauerkraut, (German)—Sour krout.
Sauerkraut, (German)—Pickled cabbage.
Saw it—Understood it.
Scatterin, Scotterin—Scattering.
Schauer, (German)—Shudder.
Schenk aus, (German) Pour out.

Schenket ein, (German)—Pour in, (fill the glasses.)
Schimmel, (German)—Grey horse.
Schimpft und flucht gar laesterlich, (German)—Swears and blasphemes abominally.
Schinken, (German)—Ham.
Schläger, (German)—A kind of sword or broadsword; a rapier used by students for duelling or fighting matches.
Schlesierwein, (German)—Wine grown in Silesia, proverbially sour.
Schlimmer, (German)—Worse.
Schlished, geschlitzt—Slit.
Schlop him ober de kop—Knocked him on the head.
Schlopped—Slopped.
Schloss, (German)—Castle.
Schnapps, (German)—Dram.
Schnitz—Pennsylvania German word for cut and dried fruit.
Schnitz, schnitzen, (German)—To chop, chip, snip. In Pennsylvania *Schnitz* or *Snits*, is applied to cut and dried fruit, apples, pears, or peaches. It was, I believe, Prof. Henry Coppée, who narrated, in Lippincott's Magazine, a story to the effect that a school teacher once asked his class if an apple were cut in two, what would the pieces be called? "Halves," replied the boys. "And if cut again?" "Quarters." "And then cut again?" "*Snitz*," was the unanimous answer.
Schönheitsidéal, (German)—The ideal of beauty.
Schopenhauer—A celebrated German "philosophical physiologist."
Schoppen, (German)—A liquid measure, chopin, pint.
Schwaben—Suabia.
Schwanen, (German)—Swans.
Schwartzer Mohr, (German)—A black negro. Mohr in German is applied very generally to both Moors and negroes.
Schweinblatt—(Swine) Dirty paper.
Schweitzer kuse, (German)—Swiss cheese.
Schwig, Swig, verb—To drink by large draughts.
Schwigs, Swig noun—A large draught.

Semysed, (German *Schmyssen,* from *Schmeissen*)—Threw him out of doors.
Scoop—Take in ; get.
Scorched—Escorted ; a negro malapropism.
Scrouged, (American)—Pressed, jammed.
Seelen—Ideal. Soul's ideal.
Sefen-lefen—Seven or eleven.
Seifenblasen—Soap balls.
Seins, (German)—The Being.
Selbstanchauungsvermögen, (German)—Capacity for self-inspection.
Serenity—A transparency.
Shanty—A board cabin ; slang for house.
Shapel—Chapel is an old word for a printing-office.
Sharman, Sherman—German.
Shings—Jingo ; by Jingo.
Shipsy—Gipsy.
Shlide—Slide. "Let it slide," vulgar for "let it go."
Shnow-wice, (German *Schnee-weis*)—Snow-white.
Shoopider—Jupiter.
Shootin-stick—Shooting stick. It is used for closing up the forms of types.
Show-spiel, Schauspiel—Play ; piece.
Shpeck—Speck, (German)—Bacon.
Shpicket—Spigot ; a pin or peg to stop a small hole in a cask of liquor.
Shpoons—Spoons ; plunder.
Shtuhl, (German *Stuhl*)—Stool ; chair.
Sinn, (German)—Meaning.
Six mals—Six times.
Skeeted—Went fast ; skated (?)
Skool—Skull.
Skyugle, (American)—"Skyugle" is a word which had a short run during 1864. It means many things, but chiefly to disappear or to make disappear. Thus a deserter "skyugled," and sometimes he "skyugled a coat or watch"
Slanganderin'—Foolishly slandering.
Slasher gaffs—Spurs for cocks with cutting edges.

Slibowitz—A Bohemian Schnapps distilled from plums.
Slop over—Go too far and upset or spill. Applied to men who venture too far in a success.
Slumgoozlin'—Slum or slum-guzzling ; humbug.
Slumgullion—A Mississippi term for a legislator.
Solidaten, (German *Soldaten*)—Soldiers.
So mit, (German)—Thus with.
Sonntags, (German)—Sundays.
Sottelet, (German *Gesattelt*)—Saddled.
Sound upon the goose—A phrase originating in the Kansas troubles, and signifying true to the cause of slavery.
Souse and Brouse, (German *Saus und Braus*)—Revelry and rioting.
Spiel, (German)—Play.
Splodderin'—Splattering.
Spook, (German *Spuk*)—A ghost.
Sporn, (German)—Spur.
Sports—Sporting men.
Staub, (German)—Dust.
Stein, (German)—Stone.
Stille, (German)—Stillness.
Stim, (German *Stimme*)—Voice.
Stohr—Store.
Straight flush—In poker, all the cards of one suit.
Strassen, (German)—Streets.
Strauss—Name of the celebrated Viennese composer.
Strumpf, (German)—Stocking.
Studenten in den Gassen, (German)—Students in the streets or lanes.
Sturm und Drang, (German)—Storm and pressure.
Sweynheim und Pannarts—The first printers at Rome.
Takes, (printer's phrase)—Allotments of copy, or strips, to each printer.
Tantzen, (German)—To dance.
Tantz, (German)—Dance.
Tarnal—Eternal.
Taub, taube, (German)—Dove.
Taugenix, Taugenichts—Good-for-nothing fellow.
Theil, (German)—Part.

Thoom—Thumb.
Thrip, (South American)—Three pence.
Thusnelda—The wife of Arminius, (Hermann.)
Tod, (German)—Dead.
Todtengrips, Todtengerippe—Skeleton.
Tofe—Dove.
To House, (German *zu Hause*)—At home.
Tortled—To tortle; to move off. From *turtle*.
Touch the dirt—Touch the road.
Treppe, (German)—Stairs.
Treu, (German)—Faithful, true.
Trow him with ecks—Pelt him with eggs.
Turner, (German)—Gymnast.
Turner Verein, (German *Turnverein*)—Gymnastic Society.
Tyfel, Teufel—Devil.
Tyfeled, Verteufelt—Devilish.
Tyfel-schnake, Teufelschnaken — Deviltries; also devil-snake.
Tyful-strikes, Teufel-streiche—Devilstrokes.
Tyful-wards—Devilwards.
Tyfelest—From Teufel: here in the sense of "best" or "worst."
Ueberschwengliche, (German)—Transcendental; elevated.
Ueber Stein and Schwein, (German)—Over stone and swine.
Ulievrus—Oliver, another of the twelve Paladins of Charlemagne who fell at Roncesvalles, (A Rowland for an Oliver.)
Und lauter guter Ding, (German)—And of thoroughly good cheer.
Urbummellied, (German *vulgar*)—Arch-loafer's song; a student song.
Urlied, (German)—The song of yore.
Van't klein komt men tot't groote, (Dutch)—Great things may have small beginnings. (Concordia res parvae cresrunt)—Legend on the Dutch ducats.
Varus—The Roman Commander in Germany, conquered by Arminius.
Verdammt, (German)—D——d.

Verflucht, (German)—Accursed.
Verfluchter, (German)—Accursed.
Verstay, Verstehen—Understand.
Vertyfeln, Verteufeln—To botch.
Verloren, (German)—Forlorn.
Versteh, verstehen (German)—To understand.
Voonderly, (German) *Wunderlich*—Wondrous ; curious.
Von—One.
Wachsen, (German)—Grow :—
    " Komm'ich in's galante Sachsen,
      Wo di schœne Maedchen wachsen."
                        Old German Song.
Waechter, (German)—Watchman.
Waelder, (German)—Woods.
Wahlverwandtschaft, (German)—Elective affinity ; sympathy of souls.
Wahrsagt, (German *Wahrsagen*)—To foretell, soothsay.
Wahres Kunstgenuss, (German)—Truly artistic enjoyment.
Waidmanncheil, (German)—Huntsman's weal, or greeting.
Ward al zu Steine, (German)—Became all stone.
Ward zu Wind, (German)—Became a wind.
Wechsebalg, (German)—A changeling ; brat ; urchin.
Weihnachtstbaum, (German)—Christmas tree.
Weiknachtslied, (German)—Christmas song.
Weingeist, (German)—Vinous ; ardent spirit.
Wein-handle, (German *Weinhandlung*)—Wineshop.
Weinnachtstraum—lit., Winenight's dream ; for " Weienacht," Christmas dream.
Wellen and Wogen, (German)—Waves and billows.
Welshhen—Turkey hen.
Werden das Werden—The becoming to be.
We'uns, you'uns—We and you. A common vulgarism through the Southern States.
    " 'Tis sad that we,uns from you'uns parts,
      When you'uns have stolen we'uns hearts."
Wie gehts, (German)—How goes it ? how are you ?
Wild Jagd—Wild hunt.
Wild un weh, (German)—Wild and woe-begone.
Wilkomm, (German)—Welcome.

Windsbraut, (German poet)—Storm; hurricane; gust of wind.
Wird, (German)—Becomes.
Wised, (German *Wusste*, from *Wizzen*)—Knew.
Witz, (German)—A sally, or witty saying.
Wo bist du? (German)—Where art?
Woe-moaedy, (German *Wemüthing*)—Moanful, doleful
Wohl, (German)—Well!
Wohl auf! (German)—Literally well up; but meaning "*hey!*" or "up there!"
Wolfsschlucht, (German)—Wolf's glen.
Wonnevol, (German *Wonnevoll*)—Blissful.
Woon, (German *Wunde*)—Wound.
Word-blay—Word-play; pun; quibble.
Wurst, (German)—Sausage.
Wurst mir und égal,—All one to me. Wurst is a German student word for indifference.
Yaeger, (German)—Huntsmen.
Yaegersmann, Faegersmann—Huntsman.
Yartausend, Jahrtausend—A thousand years.
Yartausend, Jahrtausend, (German)—A thousand years.
Yellow pine, (American)—A mulatto.
Youngest Day, (German)—Juengste tag. The Day of Judgment.
Yungling, Jüngling, (German)—Youth.
Zimmer, (German)—Room.
Zupfet aus, (German)—Tap the barrel.

www.ingramcontent.com/pod-product-compliance
Lightning Source LLC
Chambersburg PA
CBHW030249170426
43202CB00009B/684